Copyright © 2017
All rights reserved.
Printed in the United States of America.

The contents of this book are the property of Brown Technical Books, Inc. All rights reserved. No part of this book covered by the copyright hereon may be reproduced or used in any form or by any means, graphic, electronic or mechanical, including photocopying, recording, scanning, digitizing, Web distribution, information networks or by any information storage and retrieval systems, except as permitted under Section 107 or 108 of the 1979 United States Copyright Act, without the prior written permission of the author or publisher.

While every precaution has been taken in preparation for this book, the author and publisher assumes no responsibility for errors or omissions. Neither is any liability assumed from the use of the information contained herein. The reader is expressly warned to consider and adopt all safety precautions and to avoid all potential hazards. The author and publisher make no representations or warranties of any kind, nor are such representations implied with the material set forth here. The publisher and author shall not be liable for any special, consequently, or exemplary damages resulting in, in whole or part, from the reader's use of, or reliance upon, this material.

National Electrical Code ® and NEC ® are Registered Trademarks of the National Fire Protection Association, Inc., Quincy, MA.

Author: Ray Holder

Electrical Seminars, Inc.
P.O. Box 1430
Belen, NM 87002
(505) 864-3554   1-800-632-7732
www.rayholderelectricalseminars.com

TABLE OF CONTENTS

HOW TO PREPARE FOR THE EXAM...	I
HOW TO STUDY..	I
WHAT TO STUDY..	II
HELPFUL HINTS...	II
REGULATIONS AT THE EXAMINATION SITE..................................	III
TYPICAL EXAMINATION QUESTIONS..	IV
USEFUL FORMULAS	VIII
EXAM 1 – MAINTENANCE ELECTRICIAN...	1
EXAM 2 – MAINTENANCE ELECTRICIAN	7
EXAM 3 – RESIDENTIAL WIREMAN	13
EXAM 4 – RESIDENTIAL WIREMAN	19
EXAM 5 – RESIDENTIAL WIREMAN	25
EXAM 6 – RESIDENTIAL WIREMAN	31
EXAM 7 – JOURNEYMAN ELECTRICIAN	37
EXAM 8 – JOURNEYMAN ELECTRICAN	43
EXAM 9 – JOURNEYMAN ELECTRICIAN	49
EXAM 10 – JOURNEYMAN ELECTRICAN	56
EXAM 11- JOURNEYMAN ELECTRICIAN	63
EXAM 12- JOURNEYMAN ELECTRICIAN	69
EXAM 13- MASTER ELECTRICIAN	75
EXAM 14- MASTER ELECTRICIAN	82
EXAM 15- MASTER ELECTRICIAN	88

EXAM 16- MASTER ELECTRICIAN	94
EXAM 17- SIGN ELECTRICAN	101
EXAM 18- SIGN ELECTRICIAN	107
FINAL EXAM – RESIDENTIAL WIREMAN	113
FINAL EXAM- JOURNEYMAN ELECTRICAN	127
FINAL EXAM- MASTER ELECTRICIAN	145
EXAM 1 ANSWER KEY	171
EXAM 2 ANSWER KEY	173
EXAM 3 ANSWER KEY	175
EXAM 4 ANSWER KEY	177
EXAM 5 ANSWER KEY	179
EXAM 6 ANSWER KEY	181
EXAM 7 ANSWER KEY	183
EXAM 8 ANSWER KEY	185
EXAM 9 ANSWER KEY	187
EXAM 10 ANSWER KEY	189
EXAM 11 ANSWER KEY	191
EXAM 12 ANSWER KEY	193
EXAM 13 ANSWER KEY	196
EXAM 14 ANSWER KEY	198
EXAM 15 ANSWER KEY	200
EXAM 16 ANSWER KEY	203
EXAM 17 ANSWER KEY	205
EXAM 18 ANSWER KEY	207
FINAL EXAM ANSWER KEY –RESIDENTIAL WIREMAN	209
FINAL EXAM ANSWER KEY-JOURNEYMAN ELECTRICIAN	213
FINAL EXAM ANSWER KEY – MASTER ELECTRICIAN	218

INTRODUCTION

HOW TO PREPARE FOR THE EXAM

This book is a guide to preparing for the electricians' exam. It will not make you a competent electrician, nor teach you the electrical trade, but it will give you an idea of the type of questions asked on most electricians' certification examinations.

Most electrical certification exams consist of multiple-choice questions and this is the type of questions reflected in this exam preparation guide. These questions will give you a feel for how many of the examinations nationwide are structured. The questions are an example of the many questions the author has encountered when taking numerous exams in recent years.

Begin your exam preparation with two important points in mind.
  * Opportunities in life will arise - be prepared for them.
  * The more you LEARN - the more you EARN.

Attempting to take an exam without preparation is a complete waste of time. Attend classes at your local community college. Attend seminars, electrical code updates, and company sponsored programs. Many major electrical suppliers and local unions sponsor classes of this type at no cost. Take advantage of them.

Become familiar with the National Electrical Code®; the Code has a LANGUAGE all its own. Understanding the language will help one to better interpret the NEC®. Do not become intimidated by its length. Become thoroughly familiar with the definitions in Chapter One: if you don't, the remainder of the NEC® will be difficult to comprehend. Remember, on the job we use different "lingo" and phrases compared to the way the NEC® is written and to the way many test questions are expressed.

HOW TO STUDY

Before beginning to study, get into the right frame of mind. Be relaxed. Study in a quiet place that is conducive to learning. If such a place is not available, go to your local library. It is important that you have a quiet, relaxed atmosphere in which to study.

It is much better to study many short lengths of time than attempt to study fewer, longer lengths of time. Try to study a little while, say about an hour, every evening. You will need the support and understanding of your family to set aside this much-needed time.

As you study this exam preparation book and other references, highlight important points with a highlighter. This makes it easier to locate Code references when taking the exam.

Copyright © 2017

Use a straight edge, such as a six inch ruler, when using the NEC® tables and charts. A very common mistake is to get on the wrong line when using these tables: if this happens, the result is an incorrect answer.

Use tabs on the major sections of your NEC®: this makes it easier and less time-consuming to locate these major sections when taking the exam. The national average allowed per question is less than three minutes, you cannot waste time.

WHAT TO STUDY

A common reason for one to be unsuccessful when attempting to pass the electricians' exam is not knowing what to study. Approximately forty percent of most exams are known as "core" questions. This type of question is asked on most exams, and is reflected in this pre-exam preparation book.

The subject matter covered in most electrical license examinations is:

* Grounding and bonding
* Overcurrent protection
* Wiring methods and installation
* Boxes and fittings
* Services and equipment
* Motors
* Special occupancies
* Load calculations
* Lighting
* Appliances
* Box and raceway fill
* Hazardous locations
* Trade knowledge
* Electrical theory
* Demand loads

Become very familiar with questions on the above referenced subject matter. Knowing what to study is a major step to passing your exam.

HELPFUL HINTS ON TAKING THE EXAM

* <u>Complete the easy questions and "gimmies" first.</u> On most tests, all questions are valued the same. If you become too frustrated on any one question, it may reflect upon your entire test.

* <u>Keep track of time.</u> Do not spend too much time on one question. If a question is difficult for you, mark on the answer sheet the answer you think is correct and place a check (✓) by that question in the examination booklet. Then go on to the next question; if you have time after finishing the rest of the exam, you can go back to the questions you have checked. If you simply

do not know the answer to a question, guess. Choose the answer that is most familiar to you. In most cases, the answer is *B* or *C*.

* **Only change answers if you know you are right.** - Usually, your first answer is your best answer.

* **Relax** - Do not get uptight and stressed out when testing.

* **Tab your Code Book.** - References are easier and faster to find.

* **Use a straightedge.** - Prevent getting on the wrong line when referring to the tables in the NEC®.

* **Get a good night's rest before the exam.** - Do not attempt to drive several hours to an exam site. Be rested and alert.

* **Understand the question.** - One key word in a question can make a difference in what the question is asking. Underlining key words in the question will help you to understand the meaning of the question.

* **Use a dependable calculator.** - Use a solar powered calculator that has a battery back-up. Many test sites are not well lighted: this type of calculator will prepare you for such a situation. Perhaps, bring along a spare calculator.

* **Show up at least 30 minutes prior to your exam time.** - You may allow yourself even more time for traffic, etc.

TYPICAL REGULATIONS AT THE PLACE OF EXAMINATION

To ensure that all examinees are examined under equally favorable conditions, the following regulations and procedures are observed at most examination sites:

* Each examinee must present proper photo identification, preferably his/her driver's license before he/she will be permitted to take the examination.

* No cameras, notes, tape recorders, pagers or cellular phones are allowed in the examination room.

* Examinees will be permitted to work beyond the established time limits.

* Examinees are not permitted any reference material EXCEPT the National Electrical Code® book, which is permitted to be highlighted and tabbed.

* Examinees will be permitted to use noiseless calculators during the examination. Calculators which provide programmable ability or pre-programmed calculators are prohibited.

Copyright © 2017

* Permission of an examination proctor must be obtained before leaving the room while the examination is in progress.

*Each examinee is assigned to a seat specifically designated by name and/or number when admitted to the examination room.

TYPICAL EXAMINATION QUESTIONS

The examples on this page are intended to illustrate typical questions that appear on electricians' licensing exams.

EXAMPLE 1

An equipment grounding conductor of a branch circuit shall be identified by which of the following colors?

A. gray
B. white
C. black
D. green

Here you are asked to select from the listed colors the one that is to be used to identify the equipment grounding conductor of a branch circuit. Since Section 250.119 of the NEC® requires that green or green with yellow stripes be the color of insulation used on a grounding conductor (when it is not bare), the answer is **D**.

EXAMPLE 2

Driven rod and pipe grounding electrodes shall NOT be less than _____ in length.

A. 8 feet
B. 6 feet
C. 10 feet
D. 4 feet

Here the "question" is in the form of a fill-in-the blank statement. Your task is to select the choice that best completes the statement. In this case, you should have selected **A**, since Section 250.52(A)(5) of the NEC® specifies that rod and pipe electrodes shall not be less than 8 feet in length.

EXAMPLE 3

A building or other structure served shall be supplied by only one service EXCEPT one where the capacity requirements are in excess of:

A. 800 amperes at a supply voltage of 1000 volts or less.
B. 1000 amperes at a supply voltage of 600 volts or less.
C. 1500 amperes at a supply voltage of 600 volts or less.
D. 2000 amperes at a supply voltage of 1000 volts or less.

Again, the "question" is in the form of an incomplete statement and your task is to select the choice that best completes the statement. In this case, you are to find an exception. You have to select the condition that has to be met when supplying a building or structure by more than one service. You should have selected **D** because Section 230.2(C)(1) requires the conditions listed in **D** but does not require or permit the conditions listed in A, B, or C.

EXAMPLE 4

When exceptions are not a consideration, the MINIMUM size overhead service-drop conductors shall be _____ copper.

A. 6 AWG
B. 8 AWG
C. 12 AWG
D. 14 AWG

Here the "question" is in the form of "fill in the blank" and your task is to select the choice that best completes the statement. In this case, exceptions are not applicable. You have to select the minimum size conductor required for overhead service-drop conductors. You should have selected **B** because Section 230.23(B) specifies that the conductors shall not be smaller than 8 AWG copper.

HOW TO USE THIS BOOK

Practice exams numbers 1-18 contained in this book consists of twenty-five questions each. The time allotted for each of these practice exams is 75 minutes; 3.0 minutes per question. Each of the final exams varies in length, allotted time and difficulty depending on the level of test the student will be taking. Using this time limit as a standard, you should be able to complete the actual examination in the allotted time.

To get the most of this book, you should answer every question and highlight your NEC® for future references. If you have difficulty with a question, skip it and come back to it after completing the remainder of the questions. Review your answers with the "**ANSWER KEYS**" located in the back of this book. This will help you identify your strengths and weaknesses. When you discover you are weaker in some areas than others, you will know further study is necessary in those areas.

Do only one or two practice exams contained in this book during an allotted study period: this way you do not get "burned out" and fatigued. This also helps you develop good study habits.
GOOD LUCK!

Copyright © 2017

The Electrical License Process

The State of Texas has contracted with PSI Examination Services of Las Vegas, Nevada to conduct its examination program. There are currently twenty-four testing sites located throughout the state. The testing locations are at the following cities:

Abilene	Dallas	Lubbock	Tyler
Amarillo	El Paso	McAllen	Waco
Arlington	Fort Worth	Midland	
Austin	Harlingen	Richardson	
Corpus Christi	Houston	San Antonio	

Candidates may test at any of the PSI Texas testing sites. Registration and exam scheduling may be obtained at the following address:

> PSI Services LLC
> 3210 E. Tropicana
> Las Vegas, NV 89121
> 1-800-733-9267
> www.psiexams.com

Electrician license candidates may not sit for an examination without submitting a completed license application (with all required documentations and applicable fees) to TDLR. If the candidate is approved, they will be notified that they can schedule their examination. Applicants will also be informed if their application is incomplete or does not satisfy the required criteria.

The State of Texas requires an applicant for the journeyman license to have 8,000 hours (4 years) of on-the-job training under the supervision of a master or journeyman electrician and pass a journeyman electrician examination.

An applicant for the master electrician license must have 12,000 hours (6 years) of on-the-job training under the supervision of a master or journeyman electrician and pass a master electrician examination.

Information on the license may be obtained at the following address:

> Texas Electrical Licensing Board
> P.O. Box 12157
> Austin, TX 78711
> 512-463-6599
> 800-803-9202
> Fax – 512-475-2872
> Internet Address: www.license.state.tx.us
> E-Mail address: electricians@license.state.tx.us.

Complaints regarding the validity of test questions, integrity of the test and grading procedures, quality of blueprints, etc., should be addressed to the Texas Electrical Licensing Board.

ABOUT THE AUTHOR

H. Ray Holder has worked in the electrical industry for over fifty years as an apprentice, journeyman, master, field engineer, estimator, business manager, contractor, inspector, consultant, and instructor.

Mr. Holder is a graduate of Texas State University and holds a Bachelor of Science Degree in Occupational Education.

He is a certified instructor of electrical trades. His classes are presented in a simplified, easy-to-understand format for electricians. Attend one of his classes if you can, or take one of his online courses.

Since 1965 Mr. Holder has taught over 100,000 students online, in textbooks, and classrooms at Austin Community College and the University of Texas, at Austin, Texas, Odessa College, at Odessa, Texas, Technical-Vocational Institute of Albuquerque, New Mexico, Howard College, at San Angelo, Texas and in the public school systems in Ft. Worth and San Antonio, Texas, as well as conducted electrical seminars throughout the United States. He is currently the Director of Education for Electrical Seminars, Inc.

Mr. Holder is a past member of the National Fire Protection Association, International Association of Electrical Inspectors and retired member of the International Brotherhood of Electrical Workers.

Copyright © 2017

USEFUL FORMULAS

To Find	Single Phase	Three Phase	Direct Current
Amperes when kVA is known	$\dfrac{kVA \times 1{,}000}{E}$	$\dfrac{kVA \times 1{,}000}{E \times 1.732}$	not applicable
Amperes when horsepower is known	$\dfrac{HP \times 746}{E \times \%Eff. \times PF.}$	$\dfrac{HP \times 746}{E \times 1.732 \times \%Eff. \times PF.}$	$\dfrac{HP \times 746}{E \times \%Eff.}$
Amperes when Kilowatts are known	$\dfrac{kW \times 1{,}000}{E \times PF.}$	$\dfrac{kW \times 1{,}000}{E \times 1.732 \times PF.}$	$\dfrac{kW \times 1{,}000}{E}$
Kilowatts	$\dfrac{I \times E \times PF.}{1{,}000}$	$\dfrac{I \times E \times 1.732 \times PF.}{1{,}000}$	$\dfrac{I \times E}{1{,}000}$
Kilovolt Amperes	$\dfrac{I \times E}{1{,}000}$	$\dfrac{I \times E \times 1.732}{1{,}000}$	not applicable
Horsepower	$\dfrac{I \times E \times \%Eff. \times PF.}{746}$	$\dfrac{I \times E \times 1.732 \times \%Eff. \times PF.}{746}$	$\dfrac{I \times E \times \%Eff.}{746}$
Watts	$E \times I \times PF.$	$E \times I \times 1.732 \times PF.$	$E \times I$

I = Amperes

E = Volts

kW = Kilowatts

kVA = Kilovolt-Amperes

HP = Horsepower

%Eff. = Percent Efficiency

PF. = Power Factor

Copyright © 2017

Power – "Pie" Circle Formulas

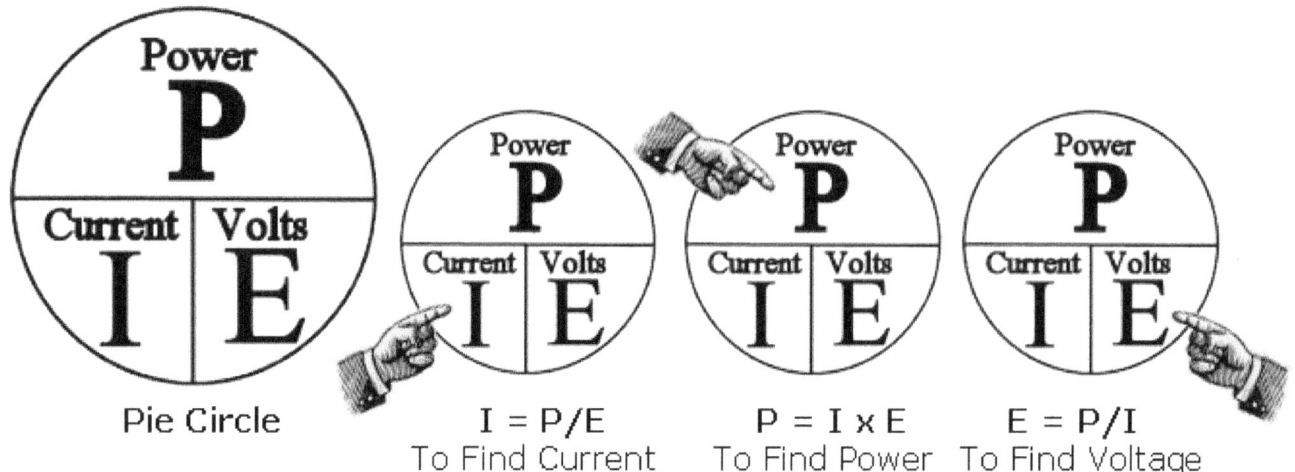

Ohms Law Circle Formulas

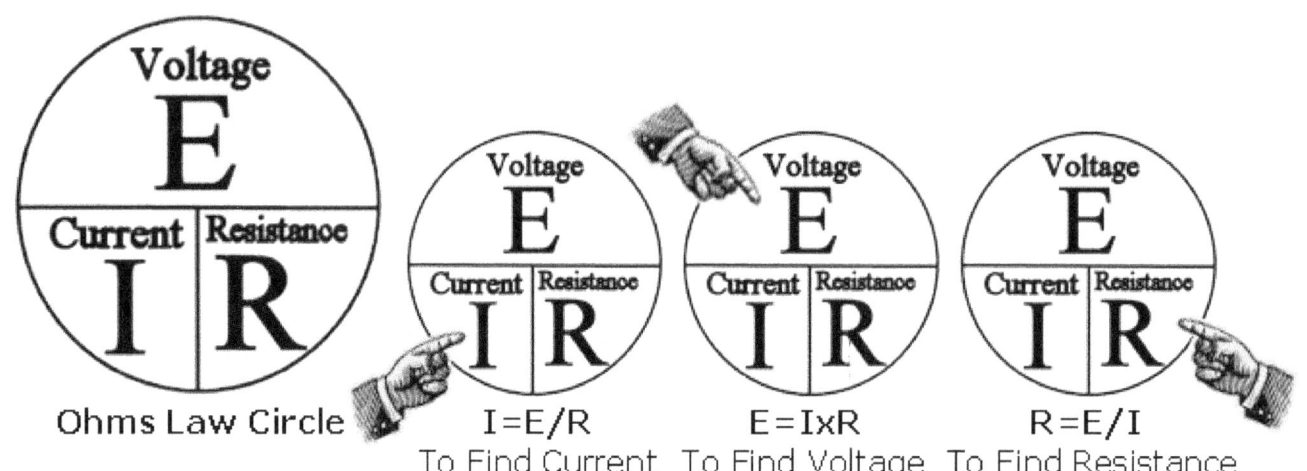

Copyright © 2017

Power Factor Triangle Formulas

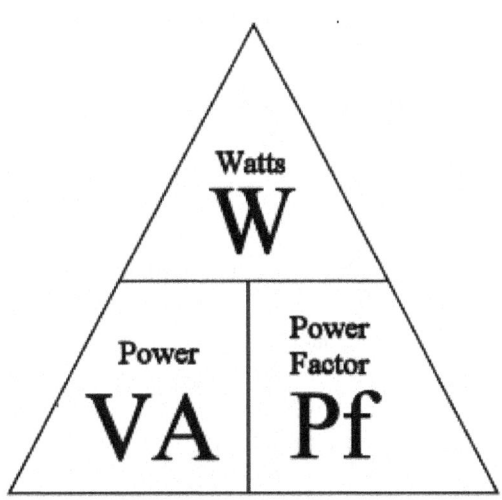

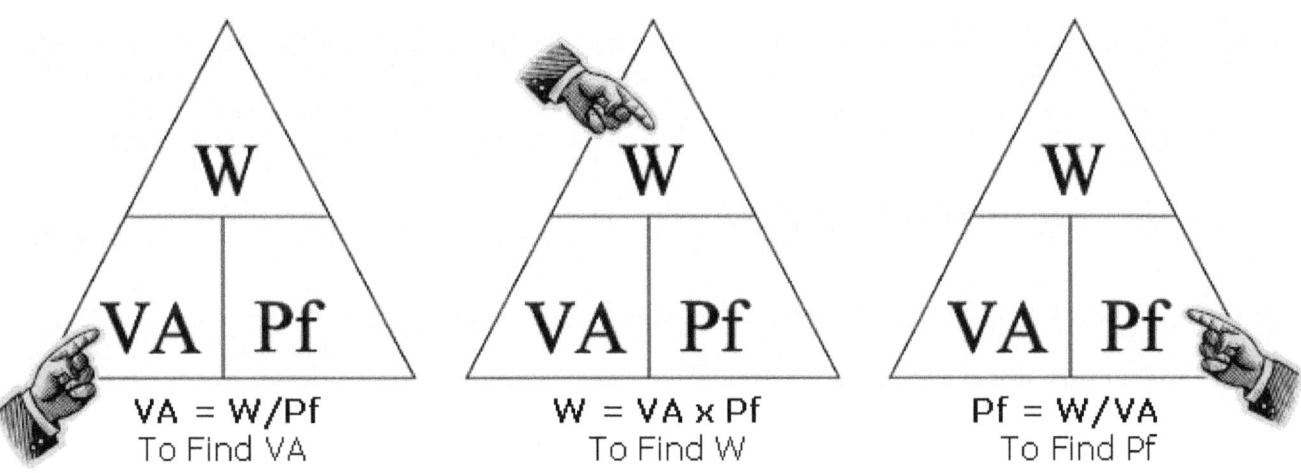

Voltage Drop Formulas

Formula Definitions:

VD = Volts dropped from a circuit.

2 = Multiplying factor for single-phase circuits. The 2 represents the conductor length in a single-phase circuit.

1.732 = Multiplying factor for three-phase circuits. The square root of 3 represents the conductor length in a three-phase circuit. The only difference between the single-phase and three-phase formulas is that "1.732" has replaced "2".

K = Approximate resistivity of the conductor per mil foot. A mil foot is a wire 1 foot long and one mil in diameter. The approximate K value for copper wire is **12.9** ohms per mil foot and for aluminum wire is **21.2** ohms per mil foot.

I = Current or amperage draw of the load.

D = The distance from the source voltage to the load.

CM = Circular mil area of the conductor. (Chapter 9, Table 8 of the NEC®)

*NOTE – When determining the wire size, distance or current, VD is the actual volts that can be dropped from the circuit. The recommended percentage of voltage drop for a branch-circuit is 3%. Example: 3% of 120 volts is 3.6 volts. DO NOT enter 3% in the VD position.

To find voltage drop in a single-phase circuit.

$$VD = \frac{2 \times K \times I \times D}{CM}$$

To find wire size in a single-phase circuit.

$$CM = \frac{2 \times K \times I \times D}{VD}$$

To find distance in a single-phase circuit.

$$D = \frac{CM \times VD}{2 \times K \times I}$$

To find MAXIMUM current in amperes in a single-phase circuit.

$$I = \frac{CM \times VD}{2 \times K \times D}$$

Copyright © 2017

Commonly used NEC® Tables and Articles:

Tbl. 110.26(A)(1)	Working Spaces About Electrical Equipment of 1000 Volts or Less
Tbl. 110.28	Enclosure Selection
210.8	GFCI Protection for Personnel
210.12	AFCI Protection
Tbl. 210.21(B)(3)	Receptacle Ratings
Tbl. 210.24	Branch-Circuit Requirements
Tbl. 220.12	General Lighting Loads by Occupancy
Tbl. 220.42	Lighting Load Demand Factors
Tbl. 220.55	Demand Factors for Household Cooking Appliances
Tbl. 220.56	Demand Factors for Commercial Kitchen Equipment
Tbl. 220.84	Optional Calculation-Demand Factors for Multi-Family Dwellings
Tbl.240.6(A)	Standard Ampere Ratings of Overcurrent Protection Devices
Tbl. 250.66	Grounding Electrode Conductor
Tbl. 250.102(C)(1)	Grounded Conductors and Bonding Jumpers for AC Systems
Tbl. 250.122	Equipment Grounding Conductors
Tbl. 300.5	Burial Depth of Conductors and Cables
Tbl. 310.15(B)(2)(a)	Ambient Temperature Correction Factors for Conductors
Tbl. 310.15(B)(3)(a)	Adjustment Factors for More Than 3 Wires in Raceway
Tbl. 310.15(B)(16)	Allowable Ampacities of Conductors in Raceways
Tbl. 310.15(B)(17)	Allowable Ampacities of Single Conductors in Free Air
Tbl. 310.104(A)	Conductor Applications and Insulations
430.32	Overload Sizing for Motors
Tbl. 430.52	Motor Overcurrent Protection
Tbl. 430.248	Single-Phase Motors Full-Load Current Ratings
Tbl. 430.250	Three-Phase Motors Full-Load Current Ratings
Tbl. 450.3(A)	Overcurrent Protection for Transformers Over 1000 Volts
Tbl. 450.3(B)	Overcurrent Protection for Transformers of 1000 Volts or Less
Chpt. 9, Tbl. 4	Dimensions and Percent Area of Conduit and Tubing
Chpt. 9, Tbl. 5	Dimensions of Insulated Conductors
Chpt. 9, Tbl. 8	Conductor Properties
Annex C	Conduit and Tubing Fill for Conductors of the Same Size
Annex D	Calculation Examples

Copyright © 2017

TEXAS ELECTRICIANS PRACTICE EXAMS
MAINTENANCE ELECTRICIAN
EXAM #1

This is an "open book" practice exam. A calculator and a 2017 edition of the NATIONAL ELECTRICAL CODE® is the only reference that should be used. This exam is typical of questions that may be encountered on the Texas Maintenance Electrician licensing exams. Select the best answer from the choices given and review your answers with the answer key included in this book.

ALLOTTED TIME: 75 minutes

1. The purpose of the NEC® is _____.

A. to have an installation that is efficient
B. the practical safeguarding of persons and property
C. for future expansion of electrical use
D. to provide an installation that is adequate for good service

2. Concealed is defined in the NEC® as being _____ .

A. not readily visible
B. made inaccessible by the structure or finish of the building
C. surrounded by walls
D. attached to the surface

3. Electrical wiring installed under canopies or roofed open porches is considered to be installed in a _____ location.

A. damp
B. wet
C. dry
D. indoor

4. Ohm's Law is a relationship between _____.

A. voltage, current and power
B. voltage, current and resistance
C. voltage, current and wattage
D. voltage, current and power factor

Copyright © 2017

5. Which of the following listed is a unit of electrical power?

A. watt
B. voltage
C. resistance
D. conductance

6. When checking for continuity between a circuit breaker and the neutral bar of a panelboard when using a continuity tester, positive continuity is indicated. The reason may be _____.

   I. a conductor is grounded
   II. a luminaire (light fixture) or an appliance may be turned on

A. I only
B. II only
C. either I or II
D. neither I nor II

7. A point in the wiring system at which current is taken to supply utilization equipment, is defined as a/an _____ in the National Electrical Code®.

A. receptacle
B. branch-circuit
C. outlet
D. circuit breaker

8. The ampacity of a conductor is defined by the NEC® to be the maximum current in amperes, a conductor can carry continuously under the conditions of use without exceeding _____.

A. its temperature rating
B. the allowable voltage drop limitations
C. its melting point
D. its rated voltage

9. As indicated in the NEC® Tables, a 3-phase, 208 volt, 10 hp, continuous-duty, induction-type motor has a full-load current rating of _____.

A. 46.2 amperes
B. 30.8 amperes
C. 55.0 amperes
D. 32.2 amperes

Copyright © 2017

10. Where a 36 in. long conduit contains one (1) ungrounded conductor, one (1) grounded conductor and one (1) equipment grounding conductor, the conduit may be filled to a MAXIMUM of _____ its cross-sectional area.

A. 53 percent
B. 31 percent
C. 40 percent
D. 60 percent

11. For the purpose of maintaining and servicing a 3-phase, 208Y/120-volt switchboard, a MINIMUM clear depth distance of ___ must be maintained in front of the switchboard.

A. 2 feet
B. 3 feet
C. 3½ feet
D. 4 feet

12. What is the largest size of insulated solid conductor permitted by the NEC® to be pulled into an existing raceway?

A. 4 AWG
B. 6 AWG
C. 8 AWG
D. 10 AWG

13. The NEC® mandates specific branch-circuits, receptacle outlets and utilization equipment to be provided with a ground-fault circuit interrupter (GFCI); this device is intended _____.

A. to prevent overloading the conductors
B. to prevent overloading the circuit breakers
C. for the protection of equipment from overloads
D. for the protection of personnel

14. Which one of the following listed circuit breakers is NOT a standard ampere rating?

A. 75 amperes
B. 90 amperes
C. 110 amperes
D. 225 amperes

Copyright © 2017

15. A 4 in. x 1½ in. metal octagon box may contain a MAXIMUM of _____ size 14 AWG conductors.

A. six
B. seven
C. nine
D. ten

16. Where exceptions are not a consideration, electrical nonmetallic tubing (ENT) shall be securely fastened at intervals NOT exceeding _____.

A. 10 feet
B. 6 feet
C. 4 feet
D. 3 feet

17. As a general rule, when an individual 20-ampere rated branch circuit serves a single receptacle outlet, the rating of the receptacle must NOT be less than _____.

A. 10 amperes
B. 15 amperes
C. 16 amperes
D. 20 amperes

18. A branch circuit supplying a 7½ hp, 240-volt, single-phase, induction-type, continuous-duty, ac motor shall have a MINIMUM ampacity of _____.

A. 60 amperes
B. 40 amperes
C. 50 amperes
D. 75 amperes

19. Refer to the previous question and determine the required size 75°C rated copper conductors permitted for use as branch circuit conductors to supply the motor.

A. 8 AWG
B. 6 AWG
C. 10 AWG
D. 4 AWG

Copyright © 2017

20. A type of fuse NOT permitted for new installations and shall be used only for replacements in existing installations is a/an _____ fuse.

A. Class K
B. Edison-base
C. Class CC
D. Time-delay

21. A 240-volt, single-phase, 10 kW commercial dishwasher will draw _____ of current.

A. 21 amperes
B. 24 amperes
C. 42 amperes
D. 30 amperes

22. A 50 ampere, 240-volt, single-phase load is to be located 150 feet from a panelboard and will be supplied with size 6 AWG copper conductors with THWN insulation. Determine the approximate voltage drop on the conductors. (K = 12.9)

A. 14.74 volts
B. 3.68 volts
C. 10.74 volts
D. 7.37 volts

23. A 40 ampere, 240-volt, single-phase, noncontinuous load is to be located 100 feet from the panelboard. If voltage drop is to be limited to 3 per cent, as recommended by the NEC®, what MINIMUM size copper branch-circuit conductors are required to supply the load? (K= 12.9)

A. 8 AWG
B. 6 AWG
C. 4 AWG
D. 2 AWG

24. Given: A 120-volt, single-phase, branch circuit is to supply fifteen (15), 150 watt incandescent luminaires (lighting fixtures) only. Determine the current in the branch circuit.

A. 36.50 amperes
B. 18.75 amperes
C. 9.37 amperes
D. 14.1 amperes

25. In general, the MAXIMUM height to the center of the operating handle of a 100 ampere disconnect switch when it is in the *ON* position, must NOT exceed _____ above the floor or working platform.

A. 5½ feet
B. 6 feet
C. 6½ feet
D. 6 feet 7 inches

END OF EXAM #1

TEXAS ELECTRICIANS PRACTICE EXAMS
MAINTENANCE ELECTRICIAN
EXAM #2

This is an "open book" practice exam. A calculator and a 2017 edition of the NATIONAL ELECTRICAL CODE® is the only reference that should be used. This exam is typical of questions that may be encountered on the Texas Maintenance Electrician licensing exams. Select the best answer from the choices given and review your answers with the answer key included in this book.

ALLOTTED TIME: 75 minutes

1. In compliance with the NEC®, a 120-volt, 20-ampere branch circuit that supplies a continuous load may be loaded to a MAXIMUM of ____ amperes or ____ volt-amperes.

A. 15 - 1800
B. 20 - 2400
C. 15 - 1440
D. 16 - 1920

2. For the purpose of maintaining electrical equipment of 1000 volts or less, the width of the working space in front of the equipment shall be the width of the equipment or NOT less than _____, whichever is greater.

A. 24 inches
B. 36 inches
C. 30 inches
D. 42 inches

3. Compliance with the provisions of the NEC® will result in an electrical installation that is essentially _____.

A. free from hazard
B. a good electrical system
C. an efficient system
D. all of these

Copyright © 2017

4. A battery charger is also a/an _____.

A. inverter
B. capacitor
C. module
D. converter

5. Which of the following is NOT required to be marked on the nameplate of a motor?

A. manufacturer's name
B. full-load current
C. overcurrent protection
D. rated temperature rise

6. Electrical equipment rooms or enclosures housing electrical apparatus that are controlled by a lock(s) shall be considered accessible to _____.

A. qualified persons only
B. electricians only
C. the building management
D. the authority having jurisdiction

7. On a 4-wire, delta-connected system, the conductor having the higher voltage to ground, (high-leg) shall be identified as _____ in color, if the grounded conductor is also present to supply lighting or similar loads.

A. white
B. red
C. green
D. orange

8. General-purpose, 125-volt, single phase, 15- or 20-ampere duplex receptacle outlets in a non-dwelling occupancy, such as an office building or a retail outlet, shall be calculated on the basis of a MINIMUM of _____ per outlet.

A. 15 amperes
B. 180 VA
C. 20 amperes
D. 150 VA

9. Where a 50 foot raceway contains nine (9) conductors and six (6) of these conductors are considered to be current-carrying, what is the derating factor that must be applied to the ampacity of the current-carrying conductors?

A. 80 percent
B. 70 percent
C. 60 percent
D. 50 percent

10. The reason the NEC® requires all grounded and ungrounded conductors of a common circuit to be grouped together in the same ferrous metal raceway is to REDUCE_____.

A. expense
B. inductive heat
C. voltage drop
D. resistance

11. In general, electrical metallic tubing (EMT) shall be securely fastened WITHIN ____ of each junction box, panelboard or other conduit termination.

A. 3 feet
B. 6 feet
C. 8 feet
D. 10 feet

12. An ac general-use snap switch may be used as a disconnecting means for a stationary motor, rated 2 hp or less, if 300 volts or less, when the motor does NOT exceed _____ of the ampere rating of the switch at its rated voltage.

A. 50 percent
B. 80 percent
C. 150 percent
D. 125 percent

13. For continuous duty-motors used in a general application, the motor nameplate current rating is used to determine the size of the _____ required for the motor.

A. disconnecting means
B. branch-circuit conductors
C. motor overload protection
D. short-circuit protection

Copyright © 2017

14. Generally, branch circuits supplying a continuous-duty, ac motor shall have an ampacity of NOT less than what percent of the full-load current rating of the motor?

A. 125 percent
B. 100 percent
C. 150 percent
D. 115 percent

15. As a general rule, an insulated equipment grounding conductor is required to have a continuous outer finish that is _____ in color and shall not be used for ungrounded or grounded circuit conductors.

A. green or green with one or more yellow stripes
B. black or black with one or more white stripes
C. white or white with one or more black stripes
D. white or white with one or more green stripes

16. When circuit breakers are used to switch 120-volt or 277-volt fluorescent lighting branch circuits, the circuit breakers shall be listed and marked _____.

   I. SWD
   II. HID

A. I only
B. II only
C. either I or II
D. neither I nor II

17. Where the premises wiring system has branch circuits supplied from more than one nominal voltage system, each ungrounded conductor of a branch circuit shall be identified by _____ at the panelboard.

A. floor
B. voltage
C. phase and system
D. room

18. No grounded conductor shall be attached to any terminal or lead so as to _____ the designated polarity.

A. change
B. reverse
C. energize
D. ground

19. Where a 9 kW, 208-volt, 3-phase electric steamer is installed in a commercial kitchen, the steamer will draw _____ of current.

A. 43 amperes
B. 4.3 amperes
C. 25 amperes
D. 75 amperes

20. What is the approximate MAXIMUM distance a single-phase, 240-volt, 42 ampere load may be located from a panelboard, where given the following related information?

   * copper conductors - K = 12.9
   * size 8 AWG THWN/THHN conductors are used
   * Limit voltage drop to 3%

A. 50 feet
B. 110 feet
C. 160 feet
D. 195 feet

21. The NEC® permits electrical trade size 3/8 in. flexible metal conduit (FMC) to be used for tap conductors to luminaires (lighting fixtures), provided the length of the FMC does NOT exceed _____.

A. 4 feet
B. 6 feet
C. 8 feet
D. 10 feet

22. Metal conduit installed in indoor wet locations such as dairies, car washes, and meat processing facilities, must have a MINIMUM airspace clearance of _____ between the conduit and the wall or supporting surface.

A. 1/8 in.
B. 1/4 in.
C. 1/2 in.
D. 3/8 in.

23. Where exceptions are not a consideration, branch-circuit conductors serving continuous loads, such as fluorescent or incandescent luminaires in an office building, shall have an ampacity of NOT less _____ of the load.

A. 125 percent
B. 115 percent
C. 150 percent
D. 80 percent

24. Where two (2) or more general-purpose receptacle outlets are connected to a branch circuit having a rating of 20 amperes, the receptacles are required to have an ampere rating of _____.

   I. 15 amperes
   II. 20 amperes

A. I only
B. II only
C. either I or II
D. neither I nor II

25. Where exceptions are not a consideration, the overcurrent protection for size 12 AWG copper conductors, regardless of the insulation type shall NOT exceed _____.

A. 15 amperes
B. 20 amperes
C. 25 amperes
D. 30 amperes

END OF EXAM #2

Copyright © 2017

TEXAS ELECTRICIANS PRACTICE EXAMS
RESIDENTIAL WIREMAN
EXAM #3

This is an "open book" practice exam. A calculator and a 2017 edition of the NATIONAL ELECTRICAL CODE® is the only reference that should be used. This exam is typical of questions that may be encountered on the Texas Residential Wireman licensing exams. Select the best answer from the choices given and review your answers with the answer key included in this book.

ALLOTTED TIME: 75 minutes

1. Wall mounted 15-and 20-ampere, 125-volt receptacle outlets installed in dwelling units shall not be counted as part of the required number of receptacle outlets where they are located MORE than _____ above the floor.

A. 18 inches
B. 24 inches
C. 4 ½ feet
D. 5 ½ feet

2. All 125-volt, single-phase, 15- or 20-ampere receptacles installed in residential garages shall be _____.

   I. protected by a listed arc-fault circuit interrupter
   II. provided with ground-fault circuit interrupter protection

A. I only
B. II only
C. both I and II
D. neither I nor II

3. All 125-volt, single-phase receptacles not exceeding 30-amperes located within at LEAST _____ of the inside walls of a hydromassage tub shall be protected by a ground-fault circuit interrupter (GFCI).

A. 4 feet
B. 5 feet
C. 6 feet
D. 10 feet

Copyright © 2017

4. Enclosed surface-mounted incandescent luminaires are permitted to be installed above the door, or on the ceiling of a clothes closet, provided there is a MINIMUM clearance of _____ between the luminaire and the nearest shelf.

A. 6 inches
B. 8 inches
C. 12 inches
D. 18 inches

5. A receptacle outlet installed for a washing machine in the laundry room of a dwelling must be installed within at LEAST _____ of the intended location of the appliance.

A. 6 feet
B. 4 feet
C. 10 feet
D. 3 feet

6. A luminaire or lampholder shall not be supported by the screw shell if the luminaire or lampholder exceeds 16 inches in any dimension or weighs MORE than _____.

A. 6 pounds
B. 12 pounds
C. 15 pounds
D. 20 pounds

7. Where a 40 gallon electric water heater to be installed has a nameplate rating of 4,500 watts @ 240-volts, single-phase, what is the MAXIMUM standard size overcurrent protection device the NEC® allows to protect this water heater?

A. 20 amperes
B. 25 amperes
C. 30 amperes
D. 35 amperes

8. Tap conductors supplying recessed luminaires shall be in a suitable raceway of at LEAST _____ in length.

A. 18 inches
B. 2 feet
C. 4 feet
D. 6 feet

9. A metal underground water pipe is permitted for use as a grounding electrode where the water pipe is in direct contact with the earth for at LEAST _____ or more.

A. 3 feet
B. 5 feet
C. 8 feet
D. 10 feet

10. Where a 175 kVA, single-phase transformer having a secondary voltage of 120/240 is installed for a multi-family dwelling, the full-load current rating of the secondary is ____.

A. 329 amperes
B. 421 amperes
C. 625 amperes
D. 729 amperes

11. When Type UF cable is installed for interior wiring, the cable must be supported at LEAST every _____.

A. 3 feet
B. 4½ feet
C. 6 feet
D. 10 feet

12. The MINIMUM number of 120-volt, 15-ampere, general lighting branch circuits required for a dwelling with 70 feet by 30 feet of livable space is _____.

A. two
B. three
C. four
D. five

13. The 125-volt receptacle outlets supplied by a 20-ampere rated residential branch-circuit are to have an ampere rating of ____.

  I. 15 amperes
  II. 20 amperes

A. I only
B. II only
C. either I or II
D. neither I nor II

Copyright © 2017

14. Receptacle outlets installed in floors of dwelling units shall not be counted as part of the required number of receptacle outlets, if they are located MORE than _____ from the wall.

A. 12 inches
B. 18 inches
C. 24 inches
D. 30 inches

15. A one-family dwelling unit is required to be provided with at LEAST _____ 120-volt, 20-ampere branch circuits.

A. four
B. two
C. three
D. five

16. The ampacity of a conductor is defined by the NEC® to be the maximum current, in amperes, a conductor can carry continuously under the conditions of use without exceeding:

A. its temperature rating.
B. the allowable voltage drop limitations.
C. its melting point.
D. its rated voltage.

17. Which of the following listed overcurrent protection devices is NOT a standard size?

A. 75 amperes
B. 90 amperes
C. 110 amperes
D. 125 amperes

18. In dwelling units, dormitories and guest rooms of hotel and motels, overcurrent protection devices shall NOT be located in _____.

A. bedrooms
B. bathrooms
C. kitchens
D. hallways

Copyright © 2017

19. As per the NEC®, a/an _____ is one who has skills and knowledge related to the construction and operation of the electrical equipment and installations and has received safety training to recognize and avoid the hazards involved.

A. knowledgeable person
B. qualified person
C. electrician
D. electrical engineer

20. Where a dwelling unit has a hallway 22 feet in length, the NEC® requires at LEAST _____ receptacle outlet(s) in the hallway.

A. one
B. two
C. three
D. four

21. In kitchens of dwelling units, receptacle outlets serving wall countertop and work surface spaces, shall be installed so that there is a MAXIMUM horizontal distance of _____ between the receptacle outlets.

A. 24 inches
B. 18 inches
C. 12 inches
D. 4 feet

22. Where you are to install a 20-ampere, 120-volt, GFCI protected, below ground Type UF cable for a branch circuit that serves landscape lighting for a residence, what is the MINIMUM ground cover required for the cable?

A. 6 inches
B. 12 inches
C. 18 inches
D. 24 inches

23. Where Type NM cable is run at angles with joists in unfinished basements, it shall be permissible to secure cables NOT smaller than _____ directly to the lower edges of the joists.

A. 10/2 AWG
B. 8/2 AWG
C. 6/2 AWG
D. 6/3 AWG

24. Where a dwelling unit to be constructed will be provided with an attached two (2) car garage, what is the MINIMUM number of 125-volt, single-phase, 15-or 20-ampere receptacles that must be located in the garage?

A. one
B. two
C. three
D. four

25. Three-way and four-way switches shall be so wired that all switching is done:

A. only in the grounded circuit conductor.
B. only in the ungrounded circuit conductor.
C. either in the grounded or ungrounded circuit conductor.
D. only in the white circuit conductor.

END OF EXAM #3

TEXAS ELECTRICIANS PRACTICE EXAMS
RESIDENTIAL WIREMAN
EXAM #4

This is an "open book" practice exam. A calculator and a 2017 edition of the NATIONAL ELECTRICAL CODE® is the only reference that should be used. This exam is typical of questions that may be encountered on the Texas Residential Wireman licensing exams. Select the best answer from the choices given and review your answers with the answer key included in this book.

ALLOTTED TIME: 75 minutes

1. In dwelling units, receptacle outlets installed for the countertops and work surfaces must be located above, but NOT more than _____ above the countertop or work surface.

A. 12 inches
B. 18 inches
C. 20 inches
D. 24 inches

2. Unless listed for the control of other loads, general-use dimmer switches, shall ONLY be used to control_____.

A. switched receptacles for cord-connected incandescent luminaires
B. permanently installed incandescent luminaires
C. a ceiling fan with a luminaire
D. holiday decorative lighting

3. The MINIMUM branch circuit rating for household electric ranges of 8.75 kW or more rating, shall be _____.

A. 25 amperes
B. 30 amperes
C. 40 amperes
D. 50 amperes

Copyright © 2017

4. The National Electrical Code® expresses conductor sizes in American Wire Gage (AWG) or in _____.

A. circular mils
B. circular diameter
C. circular centimeters
D. International Standard Gage (ISG)

5. The MAXIMUM length of flexible cord identified for use of connecting residential kitchen waste disposers is _____.

A. 18 inches
B. 24 inches
C. 36 inches
D. 48 inches

6. A two (2) gang device box is to contain two (2) size 12/2 AWG w/ground NM cables connected to a duplex receptacle and two (2) size 14/2 AWG w/ground NM cables connected to a single-pole switch. The two (2) gang box will also contain four (4) cable clamps. What MINIMUM cubic inch volume is required of the box?

A. 28 cubic inches
B. 30 cubic inches
C. 34 cubic inches
D. 36 cubic inches

7. A GFCI protected receptacle that provides power to a pool recirculating water-pump motor, shall be permitted NOT less than _____ from the inside wall of the swimming pool.

A. 5 feet
B. 6 feet
C. 10 feet
D. 12 feet

8. The grounding contacts of branch circuit receptacle outlets shall be grounded by connection to the _____ conductor.

A. bonding
B. neutral
C. grounded
D. equipment grounding

9. Any single cord-and-plug connected utilization equipment not fastened in place and where supplied by a 20-ampere, 120-volt branch circuit shall have a MAXIMUM rating of _____.

A. 10 amperes
B. 16 amperes
C. 20 amperes
D. 25 amperes

10. Where a 240-volt, single-phase, 9,600 VA electric range is installed in a residential kitchen, what is the MAXIMUM standard size circuit breaker permitted for overcurrent protection for the electric range?

A. 60 amperes
B. 50 amperes
C. 40 amperes
D. 30 amperes

11. For a one-family dwelling, the service disconnecting means shall have a rating of NOT less than _____ when supplied with a 120/240 volt, single-phase service-drop.

A. 30 amperes
B. 60 amperes
C. 100 amperes
D. 200 amperes

12. A one-family dwelling is to have three (3) wall-mounted ovens installed, rated at 6, 8, and 3.5 kW, a cooktop rated at 6 kW and a broiler rated at 3.5 kW. The MINIMUM feeder demand on the ungrounded (line) conductors is _____ when applying the general method of calculation for dwellings.

A. 12.2 kW
B. 18.6 kW
C. 27.3 kW
D. 30.1 kW

13. A conductor which is connected to establish electrical continuity and conductivity is defined as a _____ conductor.

A. grounded
B. bonded
C. grounding
D. neutral

Copyright © 2017

14. Type NM cables laid in wood notches require protection against nails or screws by using a steel plate covering the wiring. The steel plate must be at LEAST ____ thick, and installed before the building finish is applied.

A. 1/16 in.
B. 1/8 in.
C. 1/4 in.
D. 1/32 in.

15. When the ungrounded service-entrance conductors for a residence are size 3/0 AWG copper conductors, a copper grounding electrode conductor attached to the concrete-encased steel reinforcing bars used as the grounding electrode, shall NOT be smaller than size _____ .

A. 2 AWG
B. 4 AWG
C. 6 AWG
D. 8 AWG

16. Which of the following is NOT permitted for use as a grounding electrode?

A. metal underground water pipe
B. ground rod, 8 feet in length
C. metal underground gas pipe
D. concrete-encased building steel

17. A luminaire stud present in an outlet box is considered the equivalent of how many conductors?

A. none
B. one
C. two
D. three

18. When multiple Type NM cables are bundled together without maintaining spacing for a continuous length longer than _____, the allowable ampacity of each of the conductors in the cables shall be reduced.

A. 12 inches
B. 18 inches
C. 24 inches
D. 36 inches

Copyright © 2017

19. When sizing the service for one-family dwellings having a single-phase, 120/240-volt system rated 100 through 400 amperes, the ungrounded (line) service-entrance conductors shall be permitted to have an ampacity NOT less than _____ of the service rating after all demand factors have been applied.

A. 83 percent
B. 80 percent
C. 75 percent
D. 70 percent

20. The demand factor on the service and feeder conductors for six (6) residential electric clothes dryers in a multifamily dwelling unit is _____, when applying the general (standard) method of calculation for dwelling units.

A. 70 percent
B. 80 percent
C. 60 percent
D. 75 percent

21. The ampacity of Type UF cable shall be that of _____ conductors.

A. 60°C
B. 75°C
C. 85°C
D. 90°C

22. The front edge of a switch box installed in a wall constructed of wood shall be _____ from the surface of the wall.

A. flush with or projected out
B. set back a maximum of 1/4 in.
C. set back a maximum of 1/2 in.
D. set back a maximum of 3/8 in.

23. What is the MINIMUM size copper SE cable with type THHW insulation that may be used for a 150-ampere rated 120/240-volt single-phase residential service?

A. 1/0 AWG
B. 1 AWG
C. 2 AWG
D. 4 AWG

24. When a 15- or 20-ampere rated branch circuit supplies three (3) 15 ampere rated receptacles, the MAXIMUM load any one receptacle is permitted to carry is _____.

A. 10 amperes
B. 12 amperes
C. 15 amperes
D. 8 amperes

25. In general, where the opening to a lighting outlet or device box is less than 8 inches in any dimension, for the purposes of splicing or the connection of luminaires or devices, each conductor shall be long enough to extend at LEAST _____ outside the opening of the box.

A. 8 inches
B. 6 inches
C. 4 inches
D. 3 inches

END OF EXAM #4

TEXAS ELECTRICIANS PRACTICE EXAMS
RESIDENTIAL WIREMAN
EXAM #5

This is an "open book" practice exam. A calculator and a 2017 edition of the NATIONAL ELECTRICAL CODE® is the only reference that should be used. This exam is typical of questions that may be encountered on the Texas Residential Wireman licensing exams. Select the best answer from the choices given and review your answers with the answer key included in this book.

ALLOTTED TIME: 75 minutes

1. What is the MAXIMUM allowable cord length for a cord-and-plug connected built-in dishwasher installed under a counter in a dwelling unit?

A. 6 ½ feet
B. 6 feet
C. 3 feet
D. 4 feet

2. When applying the standard (general) method of calculation for dwellings, it shall be permissible to apply a demand factor of _____ to the nameplate-rating of four (4) or more fastened in place storage-type electric water heaters in a multifamily dwelling, when calculating the demand load on the ungrounded service-entrance or feeder conductors.

A. 50 percent
B. 75 percent
C. 80 percent
D. 90 percent

3. For outlet boxes designed to support ceiling-suspended (paddle) fans that weigh MORE than _____ the required marking shall include the maximum weight to be supported.

A. 20 pounds
B. 30 pounds
C. 35 pounds
D. 70 pounds

Copyright © 2017

4. A connection to a driven or buried grounding electrode shall _____.

A. be accessible
B. not be required to be accessible
C. not be permitted to be buried
D. be visible

5. In which of the following locations, if any, does the NEC® prohibit the installation of overcurrent protection devices in a dwelling?

   I. bathrooms
   II. clothes closets

A. I only
B. II only
C. both I and II
D. neither I nor II

6. The MAXIMUM number of size 10 AWG conductors permitted in a 4 in. x 1¼ in. octagon metal junction box is _____.

A. two
B. four
C. five
D. six

7. Determine the MINIMUM number of 15-ampere, 120-volt general lighting branch circuits required for a dwelling having 2,600 sq. ft. of habitable space.

A. three
B. four
C. five
D. six

8. In the load-center provided for a dwelling, how many grounded (neutral) conductors are permitted to be terminated under an individual terminal?

A. four
B. one
C. two
D. three

9. General use receptacles in a dwelling located in a living room or bedroom, shall be installed such that no point measured horizontally in any wall space is MORE than _____ from a receptacle outlet.

A. 10 feet
B. 8 feet
C. 6 feet
D. 12 feet

10. When applying the standard (general) method of calculations for dwellings, what is the demand load, in kW, for six (6) storage-type electric water heaters rated at 5 kW each installed in a multifamily dwelling unit?

A. 30 kW
B. 24 kW
C. 22.5 kW
D. 26 kW

11. In dwelling units, at least one wall receptacle outlet shall be installed in bathrooms; the outlet shall be at LEAST within _____ of the outside edge of each basin.

A. 12 inches
B. 18 inches
C. 24 inches
D. 36 inches

12. When installing NM cable through bored holes in wooden studs, the holes shall be bored so that the edge of the hole is NOT less than _____ from the edge, or the cable shall be protected by a steel plate at least 1/16 in. thick, or a listed steel plate that provides equal or better protection.

A. 3/4 in.
B. 1 in.
C. 1¼ in.
D. 1½ in.

13. Where one or more equipment grounding conductors enter an outlet box, a _____ volume allowance in accordance with Table 314.16(B) shall be made, based on the largest equipment grounding conductor present in the box.

A. single
B. double
C. triple
D. None of these, because equipment grounding conductors are not required to be counted.

14. Conductors with Type XHHW insulation may be used in:

A. dry locations only.
B. wet locations only.
C. dry or damp locations only.
D. dry, damp, or wet locations.

15. Where GFCI protection is not provided, ceiling-suspended (paddle) fans are NOT permitted to be located:

A. in a kitchen.
B. in a garage.
C. under an open porch.
D. over an indoor installed hot tub, less than 12 ft. above the water level.

16. When doing residential service and feeder calculations, electric clothes dryers are to be calculated at a MINIMUM of _____ watts (VA), or the nameplate rating, whichever is larger.

A. 3,000
B. 4,500
C. 5,000
D. 6,000

17. The rating of any single cord-and-plug connected appliance supplied by a 30-ampere branch circuit shall NOT exceed _____.

A. 30 amperes
B. 27 amperes
C. 24 amperes
D. 16 amperes

18. Where you have determined the allowable ampacity of size 12 THHN copper branch circuit conductors to be 26 amperes, what is the MAXIMUM standard size circuit breaker that may be used to protect the circuit?

A. 20 amperes
B. 15 amperes
C. 25 amperes
D. 30 amperes

19. A branch circuit supplying a 5 kW wall-mounted oven and a 7 kW counter-mounted cooktop in a residence, has a demand load of _____ on the ungrounded service-entrance conductors when applying the standard (general) method of calculations for dwellings.

A. 12 kW
B. 9.5 kW
C. 8.0 kW
D. 7.8 kW

20. The MINIMUM size copper equipment grounding conductor required to equipment served by a 40-ampere branch circuit is _____.

A. 10 AWG
B. 8 AWG
C. 12 AWG
D. 14 AWG

21. In a dwelling unit bedroom, any wall space that is at LEAST _____ or more in width must be provided with a general-use receptacle outlet.

A. 2 feet
B. 4 feet
C. 6 feet
D. 10 feet

22. Where the heating, air-conditioning or refrigeration equipment is installed on the roof of a multifamily apartment building, a 15- or 20-ampere, 125-volt receptacle _____.

A. is not required by the Code
B. may be on the line side of the equipment disconnecting means, provided the receptacle is of the GFCI type
C. shall be located on the same level and within 25 ft. of the equipment
D. may be located anywhere on the roof where the equipment is located, if the receptacle is within at least 75 ft. from the equipment

23. At the time of installation, grounded (neutral) conductors larger than size 6 AWG may be identified at its terminations by _____ colored phase tape.

A. white
B. orange
C. red
D. blue

24. The NEC® requires recessed portions of lighting fixture enclosures that are not identified for contact with insulation, to be spaced from combustible material a MINIMUM of _____.

A. 3/8 in.
B. 1/2 in.
C. 3/4 in.
D. 1 in.

25. All 125-volt, single-phase, 15- and 20-ampere receptacle outlets installed in the following locations of dwelling units, shall be protected by a listed ground-fault circuit interrupter EXCEPT _____.

A. garages
B. bathrooms
C. hallways
D. outdoors

END OF EXAM #5

Copyright © 2017

TEXAS ELECTRICIANS PRACTICE EXAMS
RESIDENTIAL WIREMAN
EXAM #6

This is an "open book" practice exam. A calculator and a 2017 edition of the NATIONAL ELECTRICAL CODE® is the only reference that should be used. This exam is typical of questions that may be encountered on the Texas Residential Wireman licensing exams. Select the best answer from the choices given and review your answers with the answer key included in this book.

ALLOTTED TIME: 75 minutes

1. A 125-volt, single-phase, 20-ampere receptacle outlet provided for the dishwasher in a residential kitchen MUST be provided with _____ protection.

   I. ground-fault circuit interrupter
   II. arc-fault circuit interrupter

A. I only
B. II only
C. both I and II
D. neither I nor II

2. The point of attachment of the overhead service conductors to a residence where the voltage is 120-volts to ground is a MINIMUM of _____ above finished grade.

A. 8 feet
B. 10 feet
C. 12 feet
D. 15 feet

3. The required MINIMUM working space, in feet, for a 120/240 volt, single-phase service when grounded parts are opposite the service equipment is _____.

A. 2 feet
B. 2½ feet
C. 3 feet
D. 4 feet

Copyright © 2017

4. Overhead spans of open conductors of not over 300 volts to ground shall have a clearance of NOT less than _____ over residential driveways.

A. 10 feet
B. 12 feet
C. 15 feet
D. 18 feet

5. The MINIMUM horizontal distance from wall switches to the inside walls of an indoor installed spa or hot tub shall be _____.

A. 5 feet
B. 10 feet
C. 15 feet
D. 12 feet

6. All 15- and 20-ampere, single-phase, 125-volt receptacles located within at LEAST _____ of the inside walls of a permanently installed swimming pool must be GFCI protected.

A. 10 feet
B. 15 feet
C. 25 feet
D. 20 feet

7. A luminaire shall be supported independently of a ceiling mounted outlet box when it weighs MORE than _____, unless the outlet box is listed and marked to indicate the maximum weight the box shall be permitted to support.

A. 6 pounds
B. 25 pounds
C. 35 pounds
D. 50 pounds

8. Of the following listed, which type of connector is prohibited for connection of a grounding conductor to equipment?

A. sheet metal screws
B. pressure connectors
C. clamps
D. lugs

Copyright © 2017

9. When driven, a ground rod is required to be driven a MINIMUM of _____ into the soil.

A. 4 feet
B. 6 feet
C. 8 feet
D. 10 feet

10. Service-entrance cables shall be supported by straps or other approved means within at LEAST _____ of every service head, gooseneck, or connection to a raceway or enclosure.

A. 1 foot
B. 3 feet
C. 6 feet
D. 30 inches

11. A receptacle outlet shall be installed at each residential kitchen countertop space or work surface that is at LEAST _____ or wider.

A. 48 inches
B. 36 inches
C. 24 inches
D. 12 inches

12. Receptacles shall NOT be located less than _____ from the inside walls of a storable pool, storable spa, or storable hot tub.

A. 5 feet
B. 6 feet
C. 8 feet
D. 10 feet

13. When grounding the structural reinforcing steel of a concrete swimming pool, what is the smallest size grounding conductor allowed by the NEC® for this installation?

A. 12 AWG
B. 10 AWG
C. 8 AWG
D. 6 AWG

14. When an intermediate metal conduit (IMC) contains conductors of 1000 volts or less and is buried under a gravel driveway of a one-family dwelling, the IMC must be buried at LEAST _____.

A. 12 inches
B. 18 inches
C. 24 inches
D. 30 inches

15. Disregarding exceptions, where residential lighting outlets are installed in interior stairways, there shall be a wall switch provided:

A. near the stairs.
B. every seven steps.
C. at the top and bottom of the stairs if there are more than six steps.
D. at any convenient location.

16. Where a 20-ampere rated branch circuit supplies multiple outlets, the receptacle outlets shall have a rating of _____.

A. 20 amperes only
B. 15 or 20 amperes
C. 10, 15 or 20 amperes
D. 15 amperes only

17. What is the MAXIMUM number of times a wire-type grounding electrode conductor is permitted to be spliced by the use of listed split-bolt connectors?

A. one
B. two
C. three
D. none

18. Where a one-family dwelling has a single-phase, 240-volt, 12 kW rated electric range installed, as per the NEC®, what would be the MINIMUM size branch circuit rating permitted?

A. 45 amperes
B. 40 amperes
C. 35 amperes
D. 30 amperes

Copyright © 2017

19. Interior metal water piping located MORE than _____ from the point of entrance to the building shall not be used as part of the grounding electrode system or as a conductor to interconnect electrodes that are part of the grounding electrode system.

A. 5 feet
B. 6 feet
C. 8 feet
D. 10 feet

20. What is the MINIMUM number of general-use receptacle outlets that must be located in a residential kitchen island countertop with a long dimension of 48 inches and 18 inches wide?

A. none
B. one
C. two
D. three

21. In general, a panelboard that houses overcurrent devices is prohibited to be installed in which one of the following locations?

A. Above a wood floor.
B. Above a carpeted area.
C. Over steps of a stairway.
D. In a concrete basement.

22. For the purpose of determining box fill, size 12 AWG THWN copper conductors are to be calculated at _____ per conductor.

A. 1.75 cubic inches
B. 2.00 cubic inches
C. 2.25 cubic inches
D. 2.50 cubic inches

23. What is the MAXIMUM distance allowed between supports when installing Type NM cable?

A. 3 feet
B. 4½ feet
C. 6 feet
D. 8 feet

Copyright © 2017

24. GFCI protection is required for personnel where a single-phase, 125-volt, 15- or 20-ampere receptacle is located above the countertop of a wet bar, if within at LEAST _____ of the outside edge of the sink.

A. 15 feet
B. 12 feet
C. 10 feet
D. 6 feet

25. How many size 12/2 AWG with ground, Type NM cables are permitted to be installed in an outlet box with a volume of 18 cubic inches that will have a duplex receptacle installed in the box?

A. one
B. two
C. three
D. four

END OF EXAM #6

Copyright © 2017

TEXAS ELECTRICIANS PRACTICE EXAMS
JOURNEYMAN ELECTRICIAN
EXAM #7

This is an "open book" practice exam. A calculator and a 2017 edition of the NATIONAL ELECTRICAL CODE® is the only reference that should be used. This exam is typical of questions that may be encountered on the Texas Journeyman Electrician licensing exams. Select the best answer from the choices given and review your answers with the answer key included in this book.

ALLOTTED TIME: 75 minutes

1. When determining the initial standard size time-delay fuses for branch-circuit, short-circuit and ground-fault protection for a three-phase, continuous-duty, squirrel cage, ac motor, the fuses shall have a rating _____ of the FLC of the motor. When the value determined does not correspond to a standard ampere rating, the next higher standard rating shall be permitted.

A. 175 percent
B. 150 percent
C. 225 percent
D. 250 percent

2. General use snap switches supplying inductive loads, shall be loaded to NO more than _____ of the ampere rating of the switch at the applied voltage.

A. 50 percent
B. 60 percent
C. 75 percent
D. 80 percent

3. A junction box to be installed will contain five (5) size 12 AWG conductors and six (6) size 10 AWG conductors. The junction box is required to have a volume of at LEAST _____.

A. 21.00 cu. in.
B. 22.75 cu. in.
C. 24.75 Cu. in.
D. 26.25 cu. in.

Copyright © 2017

4. Regardless of the voltage, the MINIMUM clearance above a diving platform of a swimming pool and messenger supported service-drop conductors is _____.

A. 14½ feet
B. 22½ feet
C. 19 feet
D. 21 feet

5. Lampholders installed over highly combustible material shall be of the _____ type.

A. IC
B. switched
C. unswitched
D. industrial

6. When installing rigid metal conduit (RMC), the NEC® requires the MAXIMUM distance between supports for trade size 2 in. RMC with threaded fittings to be:

A. 3 feet.
B. 5 feet.
C. 10 feet.
D. 16 feet.

7. For the purpose of calculating the general lighting load for a dwelling unit, the floor area should include all of the following EXCEPT _____

A. kitchens
B. bathrooms
C. an unfinished basement intended for future living space
D. an open porch not adaptable for future use

8. Where the NEC® specifies that one equipment shall be "within sight from" or "within sight of" another equipment, the specified equipment is to be visible and NOT more than _____ from the other.

A. 50 feet
B. 100 feet
C. 125 feet
D. 200 feet

Copyright © 2017

9. For nonshielded conductors of over 1000 volts, the conductor shall not be bent to a radius of LESS than _____ times the overall conductor diameter.

A. six
B. eight
C. ten
D. twelve

10. Where rigid metal conduit (RMC) or intermediate metal conduit (IMC) is threaded in the field where corrosion protection is necessary, the threads shall be coated with a/an _____ compound.

A. corrosion-proof
B. judged suitable-corrosion-resistant
C. approved electrically conductive, corrosion resistant
D. oil and tar based

11. The MAXIMUM distance between supports for trade size 1 in. rigid polyvinyl chloride (PVC) conduit shall NOT exceed _____.

A. three feet
B. four feet
C. six feet
D. ten feet

12. Determine the conductor allowable ampacity given the following related information:

　* ambient temperature - 44 deg. C
　* conductor size - 250 kcmil copper
　* conductor insulation - THWN
　* four (4) current-carrying conductors in the raceway
　* length of raceway - 125 feet

A. 160 amperes
B. 167 amperes
C. 200 amperes
D. 209 amperes

13. Disregarding exceptions, the MINIMUM size grounded or ungrounded conductors permitted to be connected in parallel (electrically joined at both ends) is _____.

A. 6 AWG
B. 1 AWG
C. 1/0 AWG
D. 2/0 AWG

14. Where a surface-mounted luminaire containing a ballast, transformer, LED driver, or power supply is to be installed on combustible low-density cellulose fiberboard, it shall be marked for this condition or shall be spaced NOT less than _____ from the surface of the fiberboard.

A. 3/4 in.
B. 1 in.
C. 1¼ in.
D. 1½ in.

15. Busways shall be securely supported at intervals NOT exceeding _____ unless otherwise designed and marked.

A. 5 feet
B. 6 feet
C. 8 feet
D. 10 feet

16. For installation in a Class II, Division 1 hazardous location, which one of the following wiring methods would NOT be approved?

A. flexible connections
B. threaded boxes
C. dusttight boxes
D. electrical metallic tubing (EMT)

17. Which of the following statements, if any, is/are true regarding the overcurrent protection of busways?

I. A busway rated for 1,800 amperes is permitted to be protected with a 2,000 ampere rated circuit breaker or fuse.
II. A busway rated for 1,400 amperes is permitted to be protected with a 1,200 ampere rated circuit breaker or fuse.

A. I only
B. II only
C. both I and II
D. neither I nor II

18. In general, when sizing the overcurrent protection, disconnect size and the supply circuit conductors for a motor used in a continuous-duty application, they shall be sized based on the:

A. full-load running current of the motor given in the Tables of the NEC®.
B. actual current marked on the motor nameplate.
C. locked-rotor current.
D. starting current of the motor.

19. Where a metal raceway protects the grounding electrode conductor between the enclosure for the main disconnect and the grounding electrode, what is the MINIMUM bonding requirements for this grounding electrode raceway?

A. It is effectively bonded by the conductor.
B. It requires a bonding jumper to the grounding electrode conductor only where it enters the panelboard.
C. It requires a bonding jumper to the grounding electrode conductor only near the grounding electrode.
D. It requires a bonding jumper to the grounding electrode at both ends of the raceway.

20. Underground installed service-conductors emerging from ground extending up a pole, shall be protected from mechanical injury up to a height of at LEAST _____ above finished grade.

A. 8 feet
B. 10 feet
C. 12 feet
D. 15 feet

Copyright © 2017

21. Receptacles supplying power to freestanding-type office furnishings shall be located NOT more than _____ from the furnishing that is connected to it.

A. 6 feet
B. 3 feet
C. 1 foot
D. 8 feet

22. Each receptacle of dc plugging boxes in motion picture studios shall be rated at NOT less than _____.

A. 50 amperes
B. 30 amperes
C. 15 amperes
D. 20 amperes

23. What is the MAXIMUM overcurrent protection rating allowed on infrared heating lamps used for commercial or industrial applications?

A. 30 amperes
B. 40 amperes
C. 50 amperes
D. 60 amperes

24. Continuous-duty motors, more than 1 hp, with a marked service factor not less than 1.15, shall have the running overload protection sized to trip at NO more than _____ of the nameplate rating of the motor, where the overload device allows the motor to start and run without tripping.

A. 115 percent
B. 125 percent
C. 130 percent
D. 140 percent

25. Disregarding exceptions, what is the MINIMUM number of overload units required by the NEC® to protect a 3-phase motor?

A. four
B. one
C. two
D. three

END OF EXAM # 7

Copyright © 2017

TEXAS ELECTRICIANS PRACTICE EXAMS
JOURNEYMAN ELECTRICIAN
EXAM #8

This is an "open book" practice exam. A calculator and a 2017 edition of the NATIONAL ELECTRICAL CODE® is the only reference that should be used. This exam is typical of questions that may be encountered on the Texas Journeyman Electrician licensing exams. Select the best answer from the choices given and review your answers with the answer key included in this book.

ALLOTTED TIME: 75 minutes

1. Where installed indoors, unless specifically listed for the purpose and location, the coupling means of the electric vehicle supply equipment shall be located at a height of NOT less than _____ above the floor.

A. 12 inches
B. 18 inches
C. 24 inches
D. 36 inches

2. For continuous-duty motors, the motor nameplate current rating is used to determine the size of the _____ required for the motor.

A. disconnecting means
B. branch-circuit conductors
C. motor overload protection
D. short-circuit protection

3. In an unvented commercial major repair garage for vehicles, the area up to a level of 18 inches above the floor is classified as _____ locations.

A. Class I, Division 1
B. Class I, Division 2
C. Class II, Division 1
D. Class II, Division 2

Copyright © 2017

4. The branch-circuit conductors supplying a continuous-duty ac motor shall have an ampacity of NOT less than what percent of the motors full-load current rating?

A. 115 percent
B. 125 percent
C. 100 percent
D. 150 percent

5. The MAXIMUM rating of the branch-circuit, short-circuit and ground-fault protective device, for a three-phase motor other than a wound rotor motor, when using an inverse time circuit breaker is _____ where exceptions are not permitted to be applied.

A. 300 percent
B. 175 percent
C. 800 percent
D. 250 percent

6. Where conductors are installed in enclosures or conduits buried underground, the interior of the enclosures or conduits shall be considered to be a _____.

A. dry location
B. damp location
C. hazardous location
D. wet location

7. An attachment plug-and-receptacle or cord connector may be permitted to serve as a motor controller if the motor is portable and has a MAXIMUM rating of _____.

A. 1/8 hp
B. 1/4 hp
C. 1/2 hp
D. 1/3 hp

8. Determine the MINIMUM required ampacity of the conductors to serve a continuous-duty, Design B, 3-phase, 208-volt, 10 hp, induction-type ac motor.

A. 30.8 amperes
B. 46.2 amperes
C. 38.5 amperes
D. 32.2 amperes

Copyright © 2017

9. Luminaires installed under metal-corrugated sheet roofing decking shall be installed and supported so there is NOT less than _____ clearance from the roof decking to the top of the luminaires.

A. 1 inch
B. 1¼ inches
C. 1½ inches
D. 2 inches

10. Fastened in place utilization equipment, other than luminaires, that is connected to a branch circuit with other loads shall NOT exceed _____ of the branch circuit rating.

A. 50 percent
B. 75 percent
C. 80 percent
D. 100 percent

11. When conduit or tubing nipples having a MAXIMUM length not to exceed _____ are installed between boxes and similar enclosures, the nipples shall be permitted to be filled to 60 percent of their cross-sectional area.

A. 6 feet
B. 12 inches
C. 18 inches
D. 24 inches

12. In regard to a dwelling unit, which of the following outlets are permitted to be connected to the 120-volt, 20-ampere branch circuit provided to supply the receptacle outlets in an attached garage?

A. readily accessible outdoor receptacle outlets
B. wall-mounted luminaires on the exterior of the garage
C. ceiling-mounted luminaires in the interior of the garage
D. all of these

13. A device box is to contain four (4) size 10 AWG conductors and four (4) size 12 AWG conductors. Assuming each conductor carries current, for the purposes of determining box fill, these conductors are equivalent to _____.

A. 17 cubic inches
B. 18 cubic inches
C. 19 cubic inches
D. 20 cubic inches

14. In general, 4 inch wide flat-top underfloor raceways shall have a covering of wood or concrete of NOT less than _____ above the raceway.

A. ½ in.
B. ¾ in.
C. 1 in.
D. 1¼ in.

15. In compliance with the NEC®, a 3 in. x 2 in. x 1½ in. metal device box may contain NO more than _____ size 12 AWG conductors.

A. three
B. four
C. five
D. six

16. When conductors are installed in a conduit or tubing nipple of_____ or less in length, the ampacity adjustment factors for more than three (3) current-carrying conductors need not be applied.

A. 24 inches
B. 30 inches
C. 32 inches
D. 6 feet

17. Circuit breakers rated at _____ or less and 1000 volts or less shall have the ampere rating molded, stamped, etched or similarly marked into their handles or escutcheon area.

A. 600 amperes
B. 200 amperes
C. 100 amperes
D. 50 amperes

18. Which of the following listed 600 volt conductor insulations have a temperature rating of 90 degrees C?

A. RH
B. RHW
C. THHN
D. TW

19. Flat conductor cable (FCC) is designed for installations under _____.

A. tile
B. carpet
C. carpet squares
D. concrete

20. An overhead feeder is to be attached to a residential garage. The conductors are insulated, have a voltage to ground of 120, and do not pass over a sidewalk or driveway. What is the MINIMUM height above the ground that must be maintained?

A. 8 feet
B. 10 feet
C. 12 feet
D. 15 feet

21. A type of conductor insulation approved for use in both dry and wet locations is _____.

A. TFE
B. THHN
C. THWN
D. SA

22. Disregarding exceptions, the NEC® mandates the MINIMUM size overhead service conductors to be _____.

A. 1 AWG copper or 2 AWG aluminum
B. 6 AWG copper or 4 AWG aluminum
C. 8 AWG copper or 6 AWG aluminum
D. 1/0 AWG copper or 2/0 AWG aluminum

23. Given: A large switchboard is to be installed in an electrical equipment room of a school. In general, if the switchboard is rated _____ or more and over 6 ft. wide, the equipment room is required to have two (2) entrances.

A. 400 amperes
B. 800 amperes
C. 1200 amperes
D. 1600 amperes

24. The workspace in front of electrical equipment such as panelboards, switchboards and motor control centers rated 1000 volts or less, shall be at LEAST _____ wide or the width of the equipment whichever is greater

A. 12 inches
B. 15 inches
C. 18 inches
D. 30 inches

25. Luminaires mounted in walls of permanently installed swimming pools shall be installed with the top of the luminaire lens NOT less than _____ below the normal water level of the pool, unless the luminaire is listed and identified for use at a lesser depth.

A. 18 inches
B. 6 inches
C. 24 inches
D. 12 inches

END OF EXAM #8

TEXAS ELECTRICIANS PRACTICE EXAMS
JOURNEYMAN ELECTRICIAN
EXAM #9

This is an "open book" practice exam. A calculator and a 2017 edition of the NATIONAL ELECTRICAL CODE® is the only reference that should be used. This exam is typical of questions that may be encountered on the Texas Journeyman Electrician licensing exams. Select the best answer from the choices given and review your answers with the answer key included in this book.

ALLOTTED TIME: 75 minutes

1. Which of the following motor controller enclosure types is NOT permitted in an outdoor location where subject to exposure to windblown dust?

A. Type 3
B. Type 3S
C. Type 3R
D. Type 3X

2. Given: A single-family dwelling with a 200 ampere, 120/240 volt, single-phase main service panel is being supplied with size 2/0 THW copper ungrounded service-entrance conductors in rigid metal conduit (RMC). The MINIMUM allowable size of the supply side bonding jumper required for this service-entrance conduit is _____.

A. 6 AWG
B. 4 AWG
C. 2 AWG
D. 1/0 AWG

3. A disconnect switch installed in a Class II, Division 2 location shall be _____ or otherwise identified for the location.

A. dusttight
B. heavy-duty type
C. raintight
D. general-duty type

Copyright © 2017

4. Disregarding exceptions, conductors installed in parallel (electrically joined at both ends) must be _____.

   I. the same length
   II. the same size

A. I only
B. II only
C. both I and II
D. neither I nor II

5. Determine the MAXIMUM allowable current-carrying capacity of a size 1/0 AWG THW copper conductor installed in a common raceway with three (3) other current carrying conductors of the same size and insulation where the ambient temperature is 86 degrees F.

A. 150 amperes
B. 105 amperes
C. 112 amperes
D. 120 amperes

6. A transformer to be installed is to supply a 243 ampere, 208-volt, 3-phase load. The transformer must have a kVA rating of at LEAST _____.

A. 300 kVA
B. 150 kVA
C. 112½ kVA
D. 90 kVA

7. Determine the MAXIMUM initial standard size nontime delay fuses permitted for branch-circuit, short-circuit and ground-fault protection for a 5 hp, 240-volt, single-phase, ac continuous-duty motor with no code letter indicated on the nameplate.

A. 60 amperes
B. 75 amperes
C. 80 amperes
D. 90 amperes

Copyright © 2017

8. When a conductor has a computed ampacity of 75 amperes, the MAXIMUM standard ampere rating of the overcurrent protection device the NEC® permits to protect this circuit is rated _____ if this is not a motor circuit or part of a branch circuit supplying multiple receptacles.

A. 70 amperes
B. 75 amperes
C. 80 amperes
D. 90 amperes

9. A 20-ampere, 120-volt load is located 150 ft. from a panelboard and is supplied with size 10 AWG copper branch-circuit conductors with THWN-2 insulation. What is the approximate voltage drop on the conductors? (K = 12.9)

A. 1.8 volts
B. 9.5 volts
C. 7.5 volts
D. 15 volts

10. Branch-circuit conductors or feeders supplying more than one motor, are required to have an ampacity of at LEAST _____ percent of the full-load current of the largest motor in the group, and _____ percent of the sum of the FLC of the other motor(s) in the group.

A. 100 - 125
B. 125 - 80
C. 100 - 80
D. 125 - 100

11. Determine the MINIMUM trade size electrical metallic tubing (EMT) required to enclose eight (8) size 6 AWG copper conductors with THHW insulation when installed in a 50 ft. conduit run.

A. 1 in.
B. 1¼ in.
C. 1½ in.
D. 2 in.

Copyright © 2017

12. Under which, if any, of the following conditions is the neutral NOT to be counted as a current carrying conductor?

I. When it is only carrying the unbalanced current.
II. When it is the neutral of a 3-phase wye-connected system where the major portion of the load consists of nonlinear loads.

A. I only
B. II only
C. both I and II
D. neither I nor II

13. As a general rule, outside open conductors on insulators, of 600 volts or less, must be covered or insulated when they are WITHIN _____ of a building

A. 10 feet
B. 12 feet
C. 15 feet
D. 25 feet

14. When a pull box contains conductors of size 4 AWG and larger and a straight pull of the conductors is to be made, the length of the box shall NOT be less than _____ times the trade diameter of the largest conduit entering the box.

A. six
B. four
C. eight
D. twelve

15. A load is considered to be continuous if the maximum current is expected to continue for at LEAST _____ hour(s) or more.

A. one
B. two
C. three
D. four

16. Cables operating at over 1000 volts and those operating at 1000 volts or less, are permitted to be installed in a common cable tray without a fixed barrier, where the cables operating at over 1000 volts are _____.

A. Type MI
B. Type NM
C. Type CT
D. Type MC

17. Which of the following listed conduits does the NEC® permit to enclose conductors feeding wet-niche underwater swimming pool luminaires?

A. electrical metallic tubing (EMT)
B. electrical nonmetallic tubing (ENT)
C. galvanized rigid metal conduit (RMC)
D. Schedule 40 rigid polyvinyl chloride conduit (PVC)

18. All of the following wiring methods are permitted in a ceiling space used as a return-air plenum EXCEPT:

A. Type AC cable.
B. rigid PVC conduit.
C. intermediate metal conduit (IMC).
D. Type MI cable.

19. When sizing the overcurrent protection for a single non-motor operated appliance, which of the following need NOT to be taken into consideration?

A. The length of time the appliance operates.
B. The full-load current marked on the appliance.
C. The voltage rating of the appliance.
D. Where the overcurrent protection selected is not a standard size.

20. In new installations, the MINIMUM working space the NEC® requires between a 480Y/277-volt switchboard and a 480-volt motor control center where facing each other is _____.

A. 3 feet
B. 3½ feet
C. 4 feet
D. 6 feet

Copyright © 2017

21. Which of the following listed cord types shall be permitted to be immersed in water to supply a permanently installed fountain located at an amusement park?

A. Type SJOW
B. Type SOO
C. Type SJ
D. Type SOW

22. When branch circuit conductors are installed inside a ballast compartment of a fluorescent or HID luminaire and they are within 3 inches of the ballast, the conductors shall have a temperature rating NOT lower than _____.

A. 105°C
B. 90°C
C. 75°C
D. 60°C

23. When a size 4 AWG or larger conductor enters a panelboard, which of the following must be provided?

A. A bonding jumper.
B. A grounding clip.
C. An insulated bushing.
D. An insulated grounding conductor.

24. Class _____ locations are those that are hazardous because of the presence of easily ignitible fibers or where materials producing combustible materials are handled, manufactured, or used.

A. I
B. II
C. III
D. IV

25. A size 2 AWG copper conductor having a temperature rating of 75 deg. C has an allowable ampacity of _____ when installed in an area where the ambient temperature is expected to reach 100 deg. F.

A. 101 amperes
B. 110 amperes
C. 115 amperes
D. 84 amperes

END OF EXAM #9

TEXAS ELECTRICIANS PRACTICE EXAMS
JOURNEYMAN ELECTRICIAN
EXAM #10

This is an "open book" practice exam. A calculator and a 2017 edition of the NATIONAL ELECTRICAL CODE® is the only reference that should be used. This exam is typical of questions that may be encountered on the Texas Journeyman Electrician licensing exams. Select the best answer from the choices given and review your answers with the answer key included in this book.

ALLOTTED TIME: 75 minutes

1. Wiring located above heated ceilings, shall be spaced not less than two (2) inches above the heated ceiling, and shall be assumed as operating at an ambient temperature of _____ ,if thermal insulation at least 2 inches thick is not located under the wiring.

A. 90°F
B. 122°F
C. 110°F
D. 86°C

2. Electrical equipment and materials included in a lists published by an organization that is acceptable to the authority having jurisdiction or has been tested and found suitable for a specific purpose, is defined in the NEC® to be _____.

A. labeled
B. identified
C. suitable for the condition of use
D. listed

3. Before demand factors are taken into consideration, for commercial buildings, general-purpose receptacle loads are to be computed at NOT less than _____ per duplex receptacle outlet.

A. 100 VA
B. 180 VA
C. 150 VA
D. 120 VA

Copyright © 2017

4. Given: A sink is installed on an island countertop in the kitchen of a dwelling. The depth of the countertop behind the sink is less than 12 inches. There is three (3) feet of countertop workspace on each side of the sink. How many single-phase, 125-volt, 15- or 20-ampere receptacles are required to be install on the island countertop?

A. one
B. two
C. three
D. four

5. Where a permanently installed generator is installed as a separately derived system, which of the following must be provided?

A. main bonding jumper
B. system bonding jumper
C. one grounding electrode only
D. multiple grounding electrodes

6. Conduit ran up to a level of 18 inches above grade at gasoline motor fuel dispensing units is to be considered installed in a Class I, Division 2 location, if it within at LEAST _____ of the gasoline motor fuel dispensing units.

A. 20 feet
B. 25 feet
C. 30 feet
D. 50 feet

7. Determine the largest trade size raceway permitted to be installed in a junction box where given the following related information:

* junction box is 12 inches in length
* conductors are size 4 AWG
* a straight pull of the conductors is to be made

A. 1 in.
B. 1¼ in.
C. 1½ in.
D. 2 in.

8. When two energized ungrounded conductors touch each other (phase to phase) due to improper insulation, this is known as a ____.

A. short-circuit
B. ground-fault
C. cross-current
D. cross-circuit

9. Given: A feeder is to supply the following continuous-duty ac motors from a motor control center:

   * motor #1 - FLC = 10 amperes
   * motor #2 - FLC = 20 amperes
   * motor #3 - FLC = 30 amperes

The feeder conductors are required to have an ampacity of at LEAST ____ .

A. 60.0 amperes
B. 75.0 amperes
C. 67.5 amperes
D. 90.0 amperes

10. What is the MINIMUM computed branch circuit load, in volt amps, permitted by the NEC® for a branch circuit serving an exterior sign?

A. 1,200 VA
B. 1,800 VA
C. 1,500 VA
D. 2,400 VA

11. Determine the MINIMUM size 75 deg. C copper conductors permitted to supply a 30 hp, 230-volt, 3-phase induction-type, continuous-duty motor.

A. 4 AWG THHN
B. 2 AWG THW
C. 4 AWG THWN
D. 3 AWG THW

12. For capacitors of over 1000 volts, a means shall be provided to reduce the residual voltage of a capacitor to _____ after the capacitor is disconnected from the source of supply.

A. 50 volts or less within 1 minute
B. 24 volts or less within 1 minute
C. 50 volts or less within 10 minutes
D. 50 volts or less within 5 minutes

13. In general, the disconnecting means for an air-conditioning unit _____.

A. shall not be located anywhere on the unit
B. shall not be located adjacent to the A/C unit
C. shall not be located on panels of the A/C unit that are designed to allow access to the unit
D. is permitted to be located on the access panels of the A/C unit, where the top of the disconnect is not within 12 inches of the top of the A/C unit

14. Given: A 4 ft. length of flexible metal conduit (FMC) with listed fittings will be installed to enclose conductors supplying utilization equipment. Flexibility will not be necessary to minimize the transmission of vibration from the equipment or to provide flexibility for equipment that requires movement. Which of the following statements regarding the FMC is TRUE?

A. An equipment grounding conductor shall be installed.
B. Regardless of the ampere rating of the overcurrent device protecting the conductors in the FMC, an equipment grounding conductor is not required.
C. The FMC is permitted as an equipment grounding conductor if the overcurrent device protecting the conductors are rated not more than 20 amperes.
D. Where the trade size of the FMC is 1½ in. or larger, an equipment grounding conductor is not necessary.

15. Given: A branch circuit supplies a single hermetic refrigerant motor-compressor for an air-conditioning unit at a dwelling unit. The motor-compressor has a full-load current rating of 18 amperes. If 30-ampere fuses used as overcurrent protection will not carry the starting current of the unit, the rating of the fuses may be increased to a MAXIMUM value of _____.

A. 35 amperes
B. 40 amperes
C. 45 amperes
D. 50 amperes

16. As a general rule, flexible metal conduit (FMC) shall be secured by an approved means at intervals NOT exceeding _____ and within at LEAST _____ of every outlet box, panelboard, conduit body or other conduit termination.

A. 3 feet - 12 inches
B. 4½ feet - 12 inches
C. 6 feet - 18 inches
D. 8 feet - 24 inches

17. For emergency systems where internal combustion engines are used as the prime mover, an on-site fuel supply shall be provided with an on-site fuel supply sufficient for NOT less than _____ full-demand operation of the system.

A. 2 hours
B. 3 hours
C. 4 hours
D. 6 hours

18. Type MI cable shall be supported at intervals NOT exceeding _____.

A. two feet
B. four feet
C. six feet
D. ten feet

19. In regard to new outdoor installations of permanently installed swimming pools, luminaires installed above the pool or within 5 ft. horizontally from the inside wall of the pool, shall be installed at a height NOT less than _____ above the maximum water level of the pool.

A. 10 feet
B. 12 feet
C. 15 feet
D. 8 feet

Copyright © 2017

20. Continuous-duty motors, rated more than 1 hp, with a service factor of less than 1.15, shall have the overload device that is responsive to motor current running sized at no more than_____ of the motor nameplate full-load ampere rating, or may have the overload protection device sized at no more than _____ of the nameplate FLA rating of the motor if the initial value selected does not allow the motor to run and start without tripping.

A. 115% - 130%
B. 125% - 140%
C. 125% - 130%
D. 115% - 140%

21. Conductors with type _____ insulation are NOT permitted to be installed in above grade raceways located outdoors where exposed to the weather.

A. THW
B. THWN
C. THHN
D. THWN-2

22. Disregarding exceptions, all 3-phase, 480/277 volt, wye electrical services, require ground-fault protection for each service disconnecting means, when rated for at LEAST _____ or more.

A. 400 amperes
B. 800 amperes
C. 1,000 amperes
D. 1,500 amperes

23. Determine the conductor ampacity given the following related information:

   * conductors are size 500 kcmil THWN copper
   * ambient temperature is 125 deg. F
   * eight (8) current-carrying conductors are in the raceway

A. 178.2 amperes
B. 199.5 amperes
C. 294.6 amperes
D. 380.0 amperes

24. The use of UF cable is prohibited by the NEC® if used _____.

A. underground
B. as service cable
C. for branch circuits
D. in attic spaces

25. Receptacles incorporating an isolated grounding conductor connection intended for the reduction of electrical noise, shall be identified by a/an _____ located on the face of the receptacle.

A. red dot
B. orange dot
C. yellow happy face
D. orange triangle

END OF EXAM #10

TEXAS ELECTRICIANS PRACTICE EXAMS
JOURNEYMAN ELECTRICIAN
EXAM #11

This is an "open book" practice exam. A calculator and a 2017 edition of the NATIONAL ELECTRICAL CODE® is the only reference that should be used. This exam is typical of questions that may be encountered on the Texas Journeyman Electrician licensing exams. Select the best answer from the choices given and review your answers with the answer key included in this book.

ALLOTTED TIME: 75 minutes

1. The lightning protection system ground terminals shall be bonded to _____.

A. the grounded terminal bar at the main disconnecting means
B. the ungrounded terminal bar at the main disconnecting means
C. the building or structure grounding electrode system
D. none of these, it shall be isolated from the building or structure

2. As a general rule, service conductors must have a clearance of at LEAST _____ laterally (to the side) from windows that are designed to be opened, doors, and porches.

A. 3 feet
B. 4 feet
C. 6 feet
D. 8 feet

3. Where used outside, aluminum grounding electrode conductors shall NOT be terminated within _____ of the earth.

A. 18 inches
B. 24 inches
C. 30 inches
D. 36 inches

Copyright © 2017

4. The connection between the grounded circuit conductor and the supply-side bonding jumper, or the equipment grounding conductor, or both, at a separately derived system is defined as the _____ in the NEC®.

A. system bonding jumper
B. equipment bonding conductor
C. grounding electrode conductor
D. neutral conductor

5. Receptacle outlets installed at a height of 16 inches above the floor in an unvented boat repair shop containing flammable liquids, are considered to be installed in a _____ hazardous location.

A. Class I, Division 1
B. Class I, Division 2
C. Class II, Division 1
D. unclassified

6. Conductor sizes addressed in the NEC® are expressed in American Wire Gauge (AWG) or in _____.

A. International Standard Gauge
B. circular centimeters
C. circular mils
D. circular diameter

7. If the grounding electrode conductor or bonding jumper is connected to one or more concrete-encased electrodes, encased for at least 20 feet, and doesn't connect to another type of electrode that requires a larger size conductor, the grounding electrode conductor isn't required to be larger than _____ copper.

A. 6 AWG
B. 2 AWG
C. 4 AWG
D. 1/0 AWG

Copyright © 2017

8. What is the MAXIMUM standard size circuit breaker that may be used for overcurrent protection for a non-motorized operated appliance with a full-load ampere rating of 20 amperes indicated on the nameplate?

A. 20 amperes
B. 25 amperes
C. 30 amperes
D. 35 amperes

9. Determine the ampacity of a size 3 AWG THHN copper conductor given the following related information:

* Three (3) current-carrying conductors are in the raceway.
* The ambient temperature is 35 deg. C.
* The terminations are rated at 60 deg. C.

A. 105.6 amperes
B. 85.0 amperes
C. 81.6 amperes
D. 110 amperes

10. Mandatory rules of the NEC® are those that identify actions that are specifically required or prohibited are characterized by the use of the terms ___.

A. shall or shall not
B. may or may not
C. will or will not
D. all of these terms apply

11. Standard electrical trade size 2 in. rigid Schedule 40 PVC conduit shall be supported at LEAST every _____.

A. 3 feet
B. 5 feet
C. 6 feet
D. 10 feet

Copyright © 2017

12. Where installed indoors, individual dry-type transformers of more than 112½ kVA rating shall be installed in a transformer room of fire-resistant construction having a MINIMUM fire resistance rating of _____ , unless specified otherwise.

A. 1 hour
B. 2 hours
C. 3 hours
D. 4 hours

13. In industrial establishments, where sizes 1/0 AWG through 4/0 AWG single conductor cables are installed in ladder type cable tray, the MAXIMUM allowable rung spacing for the ladder cable tray shall be _____ .

A. 6 inches
B. 9 inches
C. 12 inches
D. 15 inches

14. The NEC® mandates all single-phase cord-and-plug-connected room air conditioners to be provided with _____ .

A. a flexible cord not more than 6 feet in length
B. a flexible cord with conductors not smaller than 12 AWG
C. factory-installed GFCI protection
D. factory- installed LCDI, HDCI, or AFCI protection

15. Type AC cable shall provide an adequate path for _____ .

A. water drainage
B. a grounding electrode
C. fault-current
D. grounding conductors

16. The ampacity of the phase conductors from the generator terminals to the first overcurrent device shall NOT be less than _____ of the nameplate current rating of the generator where the design of the generator does not prevent overloading.

A. 100 percent
B. 125 percent
C. 115 percent
D. 150 percent

17. Which of the following circuits is prohibited for the grounded conductor to be dependent on receptacle devices for continuity?

A. All circuits.
B. Multi-outlet circuits.
C. GFCI protected circuits.
D. Multiwire branch circuits.

18. In guest rooms and guest suites of hotels and motels, at LEAST _____ receptacle outlet(s) shall be readily accessible.

A. one
B. two
C. three
D. four

19. Circuit breakers shall be permitted to be connected in parallel _____.

A. where factory assembled
B. under no circumstances
C. where the load to be supplied is not greater than 100 amperes
D. where the nominal voltage to ground is not more than 300 volts

20. Unless specifically permitted in the NEC®, a neutral conductor shall NOT be used for more than one _____.

A. branch circuit
B. multiwire branch circuit
C. set of ungrounded feeder conductors
D. all of these apply

21. Where an ac service is supplied with four (4) parallel sets of size 500 kcmil aluminum conductors, what is the MINIMUM size copper grounding electrode conductor required, when connected to a metal underground water pipe used as a grounding electrode? Assume the water piping does not extend to other types of electrodes.

A. 6 AWG
B. 4 AWG
C. 2/0 AWG
D. 3/0 AWG

22. Where an ac transformer arc welder has a 50 ampere rated primary current and a 60 percent duty cycle, determine the MINIMUM size copper 60 deg. C rated conductors required to supply this welder.

A. 6 AWG
B. 8 AWG
C. 10 AWG
D. 4 AWG

23. In general, cables or raceways shall be permitted to be laid in notches in wood studs where the cable or raceway at those points is protected against nails or screws by a steel plate at LEAST _____ thick.

A. 1/16 in.
B. 1/8 in.
C. 1/4 in.
D. 3/8 in.

24. Where one or more receptacle outlets are provided for the show window lighting in a retail store, the outlet(s) shall be installed within at LEAST _____ of the top of the show window.

A. 30 inches
B. 24 inches
C. 18 inches
D. 12 inches

25. Flexible cords and cables shall NOT be used:

A. as elevator cables.
B. when run through holes in walls.
C. to prevent transmission of vibration.
D. as information technology equipment cables.

END OF EXAM #11

Copyright © 2017

TEXAS ELECTRICIANS PRACTICE EXAMS
JOURNEYMAN ELECTRICIAN
EXAM #12

This is an "open book" practice exam. A calculator and a 2017 edition of the NATIONAL ELECTRICAL CODE® is the only reference that should be used. This exam is typical of questions that may be encountered on the Texas Journeyman Electrician licensing exams. Select the best answer from the choices given and review your answers with the answer key included in this book.

ALLOTTED TIME: 75 minutes

1. For the purpose of determining conductor fill in conduit, what is the total area, expressed in square inches, for the following combination of conductors?

   * three - size 4/0 AWG THWN
   * one - size 3/0 AWG THWN
   * one - size 4 AWG THWN

A. 1.3214 square inches.
B. 1.6380 square inches.
C. 1.8572 square inches.
D. 1.2098 square inches.

2. Which of the following listed cables has an overall covering that is fungus resistant?

A. Type NM
B. Type NMS
C. Type NMC
D. Type NM-B

3. A fused disconnecting means for motor circuits rated 1000 volts or less, shall have an ampacity of at LEAST _____ of the full-load current rating of the motor it disconnects.

A. 100 percent
B. 115 percent
C. 125 percent
D. 150 percent

4. Disregarding exceptions, where feeder conductors of not more than 600 volts supply a continuous load of 240 amperes, the conductors are required to have an ampacity of at LEAST _____.

A. 192 amperes
B. 240 amperes
C. 300 amperes
D. 276 amperes

5. Determine the MINIMUM number of 20-ampere, 120-volt general lighting branch circuits required for a 12 unit apartment building that is 12,000 sq. ft. in size. The apartment building is not designed for permanent residents and does not contain cooking facilities.

A. 12
B. 24
C. 14
D. 10

6. Where an 80 ampere, 240-volt, single-phase load is located 200 feet from a panelboard and is supplied with size 3 AWG copper conductors with THWN insulation, what is the approximate voltage drop on this circuit? (K = 12.9)

A. 6 volts
B. 4 volts
C. 9.2 volts
D. 7.84 volts

7. Enclosures installed in a Class I, Division 1 location containing components that have arcing devices must have an approved seal located within at LEAST _____ of each conduit run entering or leaving such enclosures, or as required by the enclosure marking.

A. 12 inches
B. 18 inches
C. 24 inches
D. 30 inches

8. Where installed in a common raceway, conductors of ac and dc circuits, rated 1,000 volts or less, having different types of insulation, _____.

A. are not permitted
B. shall be identified with different surface colors
C. require raceway fill limited to 40%
D. shall not have an applied voltage exceeding the lowest conductor insulation rating

9. In industrial establishments where the conditions of maintenance and supervision ensure that only qualified persons service the installation, flexible cords and flexible cables are permitted to be installed in aboveground raceways that are NO longer than _____ to protect the flexible cord or flexible cable from physical damage.

A. 50 feet
B. 10 feet
C. 100 feet
D. 25 feet

10. The NEC® requires an equipment bonding jumper installed on the load side of an overcurrent device to be _____.

A. insulated
B. bare
C. continuous
D. non-insulated

11. When bonding all metal piping systems and all grounded metal parts in contact with the circulating water of a hydromassage bathtub, the bonding conductors used must be directly bonded to _____.

A. the bonding terminal on the circulating water pump motor
B. the grounding electrode system
C. both the service and secondary panelboards
D. the grounding terminal at either the service or secondary panelboards

12. Where a building has a 208Y/120 volt, 3-phase, 4-wire service with a balanced net computed load at 90 kVA, determine the current each ungrounded (phase) conductor will carry at full-load.

A. 188 amperes
B. 250 amperes
C. 433 amperes
D. 750 amperes

Copyright © 2017

13. When a circuit breaker is used as the disconnecting means for a 20 hp, 480-volt, 3-phase, continuous-duty motor, the circuit breaker shall have a standard ampere rating of at LEAST _____.

A. 30 amperes
B. 35 amperes
C. 40 amperes
D. 45 amperes

14. Which of the following is NOT permitted in cable trays of industrial establishments?

A. Nonmetallic sheathed cable.
B. Multi-conductor service-entrance cable.
C. Individual ungrounded conductors smaller than 1/0 AWG.
D. Multi-conductor underground feeder and branch circuit cable.

15. Branch circuits supplying more than one outlet supplying residential fixed electric baseboard heaters, shall have a MAXIMUM rating of _____.

A. 20 amperes
B. 30 amperes
C. 40 amperes
D. 50 amperes

16. Where building a new indoor electrical service for a commercial or industrial occupancy, at least one (1) 125-volt, single-phase, 15- or 20-ampere-rated receptacle outlet shall be installed in an accessible location within at LEAST _____ of the electrical service equipment and in the same room or area as the service equipment.

A. 6 feet
B. 10 feet
C. 50 feet
D. 25 feet

17. Given: A dairy farm with a 120/240-volt, single-phase electrical system will have the following three (3) loads supplied from a common service, one – 18,000 VA, one – 16,000 VA, and one -10,000 VA. What is the demand load, in amperes, on the ungrounded service-entrance conductors?

A. 183 amperes
B. 152 amperes
C. 304 amperes
D. 114 amperes

18. Given: A metal junction box has a volume of 27 cubic inches and contains a total of six (6) size 12 AWG conductors. Additional wires of size 10 AWG need to be added in the box. No grounding conductors, devices or fittings are contained in the box. What is the MAXIMUM number of size 10 AWG conductors that may be added to this box?

A. two
B. five
C. six
D. eight

19. A dry-type transformer of less than 1000 volts and _____ is permitted to be installed in a hollow space of a building, such as above an accessible lift-out ceiling, provided there is adequate ventilation.

A. 25 kVA
B. 37½ kVA
C. 50 kVA
D. 112½ kVA

20. Which of the following listed is NOT required to be marked on the nameplate of an ac motor?

A. time rating
B. rated temperature rise
C. full-load current
D. overcurrent protection

21. A location in which flammable liquid-produced vapors, or combustible liquid-produced vapors are present in the air in quantities sufficient to produce explosive or ignitible mixtures is classified as a _____ hazardous location.

A. Class I
B. Class II
C. Class III
D. Class IV

22. Where a receptacle outlet is removed from an underfloor raceway, the conductors supplying the outlet shall be _____.

A. capped with an approved insulating material
B. taped off with red colored phase tape
C. marked and identified
D. removed from the raceway

23. Floor-mounted Type FCC cable shall be covered with carpet squares NOT larger than _____.

A. 18.50 inches square
B. 24.75 inches square
C. 36.00 inches square
D. 39.37 inches square

24. Equipment grounding conductors for solar photovoltaic (PV) source and PV output circuits shall NOT be smaller than _____.

A. 14 AWG
B. 12 AWG
C. 10 AWG
D. 8 AWG

25. Ten (10) copper conductors with THW insulation are to be installed in a 20 ft. length of intermediate metal conduit (IMC); five (5) size 1 AWG and five (5) size 3 AWG. What is the MINIMUM allowable trade size IMC required to contain these ten (10) conductors?

A. 1½ in.
B. 2 in.
C. 2½ in.
D. 3 in.

END OF EXAM #12

Copyright © 2017

TEXAS ELECTRICIANS PRACTICE EXAMS
MASTER ELECTRICIAN
EXAM #13

This is an "open book" practice exam. A calculator and a 2017 edition of the NATIONAL ELECTRICAL CODE® is the only reference that should be used. This exam is typical of questions that may be encountered on the Texas Master Electrician licensing exams. Select the best answer from the choices given and review your answers with the answer key included in this book.

ALLOTTED TIME: 75 minutes

1. Given: a 150 kVA service transformer has a 480Y/277-volt 3-phase primary and a 208Y/120-volt, 3-phase secondary. What is the approximate full-load ampere rating of the primary of the transformer?

A. 180 amperes
B. 312 amperes
C. 542 amperes
D. 416 amperes

2. Where a conductor is marked *RHW-2* on the insulation what does the -2 represent?

A. The cable has 2 conductors.
B. The conductor is double insulated.
C. The conductor has a nylon outer jacket.
D. The conductor has a maximum operating temperature of 90°C.

3. As a general rule for a grounded electrical system, the equipment grounding conductor for a feeder or a branch circuit shall be sized in accordance with _____.

A. the ungrounded circuit conductors
B. the overcurrent protective device
C. the service entrance conductors
D. the grounding electrode

Copyright © 2017

4. Determine the allowable ampacity of a size 350 kcmil THW aluminum conductor installed in a raceway with four (4) other current-carrying conductors when the expected ambient temperature is 44 deg. C.

A. 151 amperes
B. 164 amperes
C. 210 amperes
D. 146 amperes

5. Determine the MAXIMUM number of 120-volt, general-purpose duplex receptacles the NEC® permits to be protected by a 20-ampere, 120-volt single-pole circuit breaker in a commercial building.

A. 18
B. 15
C. 13
D. 10

6. For low voltage lighting systems operating at 30 volts or less, the output circuits of the power supply are to be rated for NOT more than _____ under all load conditions.

A. 15 amperes
B. 20 amperes
C. 25 amperes
D. 30 amperes

7. Where sub-feeder conductors less than ten (10) feet long are tapped from feeder conductors, the ampacity of the tap conductors shall be _____.

A. one-half of the rating of the overcurrent device protecting the feeder conductors
B. one-third of the rating of the overcurrent device protecting the feeder conductors
C. 125 percent of the combined loads to be served by the tap conductors
D. not less than the combined calculated loads on the circuits supplied by the tap conductors

8. Determine the conductor allowable ampacity given the following related information:

* ambient temperature of 44 deg. C
* 250 kcmil THWN copper conductors
* four (4) current-carrying conductors in the raceway
* length of raceway is 50 feet

A. 160 amperes
B. 167 amperes
C. 200 amperes
D. 209 amperes

9. Generally, the grounded conductor and the grounding conductor must be bonded together in _____ of a premises wiring system supplied by a grounded ac service.

   I. panelboards used as service equipment
   II. all sub-panels

A. I only
B. II only
C. both I and II
D. neither I nor II

10. Using the standard method of calculations, what is the demand, in kW, on the ungrounded service-entrance conductors of a multifamily apartment complex that has thirty-five (35) electric ranges rated at 11.5 kW each?

A. 403 kW
B. 15 kW
C. 280 kW
D. 50 kW

11. A grounding ring consisting of a size 2 AWG bare copper wire encircling a building, buried 36 in. deep, in direct contact with the earth, is required to have a MINIMUM length of _____.

A. 15 feet
B. 20 feet
C. 25 feet
D. 50 feet

12. Where applying the optional method of calculations for a one-family dwelling, what is the demand load for the heating and cooling, in kW, on the ungrounded service-entrance conductors for a residence that has the following?

   * one blower motor rated 1.2 kW, interlocked with both space heating and AC equipment
   * one central electric space-heating unit rated 25 kW
   * one air-conditioning unit rated 6.5 kW

Copyright © 2017

A. 32.75 kW
B. 25.00 kW
C. 17.03 kW
D. 26.20 kW

13. Apply the general method of calculations for dwelling units and determine the MINIMUM demand load, in VA, where a one-family residence has the following fastened in place appliances.

   *microwave oven - 1,250 VA
   *trash compacter - 960 VA
   *dishwasher - 1,400 VA
   *garage door opener - 960 VA

A. 3,428 VA
B. 3,656 VA
C. 4,570 VA
D. 4,883 VA

14. Generally, the NEC® mandates the conductors in outdoor conduits installed less than 7/8 in. above the surface of the rooftop are subject to a ambient temperature adder of 60°F, when the roof is exposed to direct sunlight. Therefore, the conductors are subject to temperature correction factors. An exception to this rule without having to apply an ambient temperature adjustment correction factor of these conductors is _____.

A. not permitted
B. when the conductors are rated for 90°C
C. when the conductors have Type THWN/THHN insulation
D. when the conductors are of Type XHHW-2 insulation

15. What is the MAXIMUM distance between supports for straight horizontal runs of trade size 1½ in. threaded rigid metal conduit (RMC)?

A. 10 feet
B. 12 feet
C. 14 feet
D. 16 feet

16. At least one receptacle outlet shall be installed directly above a show window of a department store for each _____ linear feet or major fraction thereof of show window area.

Copyright © 2017

A. six
B. eight
C. ten
D. twelve

17. A thermal barrier shall be required if the space between the resistors and reactors, of 1000 volts or less, and combustible material is LESS than _____.

A. 12 inches
B. 18 inches
C. 10 inches
D. 6 inches

18. In movie theaters, all switches for controlling the emergency lighting systems shall be located _____.

A. on the stage
B. in the lobby
C. in the manager's office
D. in the projection booth

19. Where a 90 ampere, 240-volt, single-phase load is located 225 feet from a panelboard and is supplied with size 3 AWG copper conductors, determine the approximate voltage drop on the conductors. (K = 12.9)

A. 6 volts
B. 4 volts
C. 8 volts
D. 10 volts

20. A listed _____ shall be installed in or on all emergency systems switchboards and panelboards.

A. LCDI
B. GFCI
C. AFCI
D. SPD

21. Given: A trade size 2 in. electrical metallic tubing (EMT) containing four (4) size 2/0 AWG THWN copper conductors is to be installed in a pull box for a straight pull of the conductors. What is the MINIMUM required length of the pull box?

A. 4 inches
B. 12 inches
C. 16 inches
D. 24 inches

22. Where multiple driven ground rods make up the entire grounding electrode system for a 1,200 ampere service, the MINIMUM size copper conductor required to bond the ground rods together is _____.

A. 8 AWG
B. 6 AWG
C. 2/0 AWG
D. 3/0 AWG

23. Conductors tapped from a feeder and supplying the primary of a transformer need not have overcurrent protection, if the length of the tap conductors are not over 25 feet and have an ampacity of at LEAST _____ of the rating of the overcurrent device protecting the feeder conductors.

A. one-third
B. one-half
C. 80 percent
D. 75 percent

24. Where conductors carrying alternating current are installed in ferrous metal raceways, _____.

A. all phase conductors, the grounded conductor and equipment grounding conductors shall be grouped together
B. the phase conductors shall not be grouped with the grounded conductor
C. the equipment grounding conductor is not permitted to be in the same raceway with the grounded and ungrounded conductors
D. the equipment grounding conductors are not permitted to be installed in a common raceway with the grounded conductors

25. All hydromassage bathtub metal piping systems and all grounded metal parts in contact with the circulating water associated with the bathtub shall be bonded together using a solid copper bonding jumper NOT smaller than _____.

A. 10 AWG
B. 8 AWG
C. 6 AWG
D. 12 AWG

END OF EXAM #13

TEXAS ELECTRICIANS PRACTICE EXAMS
MASTER ELECTRICIAN
EXAM #14

This is an "open book" practice exam. A calculator and a 2017 edition of the NATIONAL ELECTRICAL CODE® is the only reference that should be used. This exam is typical of questions that may be encountered on the Texas Master Electrician licensing exams. Select the best answer from the choices given and review your answers with the answer key included in this book.

ALLOTTED TIME: 75 minutes

1. When a service or feeder with two (2) or more disconnecting means in separate enclosures utilize a common grounding electrode conductor busbar for making conductor taps, the aluminum or copper busbar is required to be of sufficient length to accommodate the number of terminations necessary for the installation, be NOT less than _____ and shall be installed in an accessible location.

A. ¼ in. thick and 2 in. wide
B. ½ in. thick and 4 in. wide
C. ½ in. thick and 2 in. wide
D. ¼ in. thick and 4 in. wide

2. In a maintenance or storage aircraft hangar, the area that extends upward from the floor level _____ above the upper surface of aircraft wings, power plants and fuel tanks shall be classified as a Class I, Division 2 or Zone 2 location.

A. 5 feet
B. 6 feet
C. 8 feet
D. 10 feet

3. Given: After all demand factors have been taken into consideration, a small office building with a single-phase, 120/240-volt electrical system has a demand load of 35,000 watts. The MINIMUM size THW copper conductors required for the ungrounded service-entrance conductors is _____.

A. 3 AWG
B. 1/0 AWG
C. 2/0 AWG
D. 3/0 AWG

Copyright © 2017

4. Where rigid polyvinyl chloride (PVC) conduit is installed underground to supply a gasoline dispensing unit, threaded rigid metal conduit (RMC) or threaded intermediate metal conduit (IMC) shall be used for the LAST _____ of the underground run to where the conduit emerges.

A. 2 feet
B. 4 feet
C. 5 feet
D. 6 feet

5. Where electrical metallic tubing (EMT) is installed under metal-corrugated sheet roofing decking, a clearance of at LEAST _____ must be maintained between the top of the tubing and the surface of the roof decking.

A. 1 in.
B. 1¼ in.
C. 1½ in.
D. 2 in.

6. After applying all demand factors, the ampacity of the service-entrance conductors are required to be NOT less than _____ where both the overcurrent device and its assembly are not listed for operation at 100 percent of their rating.

A. 125 percent of the loads on the branch circuits
B. the sum of the loads on the branch circuits
C. the sum of the noncontinuous loads plus 125 percent of the continuous loads
D. the sum of all branch-circuit overcurrent protection devices

7. Electrical services and feeders supplying electrified truck parking spaces in a truck plaza shall be calculated on the basis of NOT less than _____ per electrified truck parking space.

A. 11 kVA
B. 8½ kVA
C. 12 kVA
D. 8 watts per sq. ft. of parking space

8. The accessible portion of abandoned supply circuits and interconnecting cables located in an information technology equipment room shall be removed, UNLESS _____.

A. tagged and identified as abandoned
B. identified as Type CMP
C. contained in a raceway
D. disconnected from their supply source

Copyright © 2017

9. A residential branch circuit is to supply two (2) wall-mounted ovens rated at 4 kW each and one (1) 6 kW counter-mounted cooktop. Where all the equipment is 240 volts, single-phase, the branch-circuit conductors supplying this kitchen equipment shall have an ampacity of at LEAST _____.

A. 22 amperes
B. 27 amperes
C. 33 amperes
D. 37 amperes

10. Where permanently mounted luminaires in a commercial garage are located over lanes on which vehicles are commonly driven, the luminaires shall be installed NOT less than _____ above the floor level, unless of the totally enclosed type or constructed so as to prevent escape of sparks or hot metal particles.

A. 10 feet
B. 12 feet
C. 14 feet
D. 16 feet

11. What MINIMUM size THWN copper conductors are required to supply a continuous-duty, 25 hp, 208-volt, 3-phase motor? Given: The motor is on the end of a short conduit run that contains only three (3) conductors at an ambient temperature of 50 deg. C. Consider the motor terminations to be rated for 75°C.

A. 6 AWG
B. 3 AWG
C. 2 AWG
D. 1 AWG

12. GFCI protection is required for all receptacles located within what MINIMUM distance, in feet, of a therapeutic tub?

A. 3 feet
B. 6 feet
C. 10 feet
D. 12 feet

Copyright © 2017

13. Portable lampholders used in a commercial service and repair garage shall NOT be equipped with a _____.

A. switch
B. nonconductive handle
C. hook
D. protective guard of nonconductive material

14. The emergency controls for attended self-service gasoline stations and convenience stores with motor fuel dispensers must be located NOT more than _____ from the motor fuel dispensers.

A. 20 feet
B. 50 feet
C. 75 feet
D. 100 feet

15. Which of the following listed wiring methods is NOT approved for use in assembly locations, UNLESS encased in concrete?

A. EMT
B. Schedule 80 PVC
C. Type MC cable
D. Type AC cable

16. Where transformer vaults are not protected with an automatic fire-suppression system, they shall be constructed of materials that have a MINIMUM fire-resistance rating of _____.

A. 1 hour
B. 2 hours
C. 3 hours
D. 4 hours

17. What percent of electrical supplied spaces in a recreational vehicle park must have 30-ampere, 125-volt receptacle outlets provided?

A. 60 percent
B. 70 percent
C. 90 percent
D. 100 percent

Copyright © 2017

18. What is the MINIMUM bend radius of trade size 4 in. rigid metal conduit (RMC) where the bend is not made with a one-shot or full-shoe bender?

A. 16 inches
B. 18 inches
C. 24 inches
D. 30 inches

19. The voltage rating of electrical equipment shall NOT be less than the ____ to which it is connected.

A. nominal voltage of the circuit
B. overcurrent protection
C. service-entrance voltage
D. load

20. Where portions of a cable, raceway or sleeve are known to be subjected to different temperatures and where condensation is known to be a problem, the raceway or sleeve shall _____.

A. be filled with an approved material
B. have an explosionproof seal
C. be provided with a drain
D. be installed below the level of the terminations

21. What is the MINIMUM size 75°C copper service-entrance conductors required for a 200 ampere rated commercial service?

A. 4/0 THW
B. 2/0 THW
C. 3/0 THHN
D. 3/0 THW

22. Determine the MINIMUM size THWN copper feeder conductors required by the NEC® to supply the following 480-volt, continuous duty, 3-phase, induction type, Design B, motors.

* 1 – 40 hp
* 1 – 50 hp
* 1 – 60 hp

A. 2/0 AWG
B. 3/0 AWG
C. 4/0 AWG
D. 250 kcmil

23. Two (2) or more motors may be installed without individual overcurrent protection devices if rated less than 1 hp each, and the full-load current rating of each motor does NOT exceed _____, if they are on a 120-volt, 20-ampere branch circuit.

A. 2 amperes
B. 4 amperes
C. 5 amperes
D. 6 amperes

24. Where a listed packaged spa or hot tub is installed outdoors, the unit is permitted to be cord-and-plug connected, provided the cord is NOT longer than _____ and protected by a GFCI.

A. 6 feet
B. 10 feet
C. 15 feet
D. 20 feet

25. Given: A three-phase, 480-volt, 100 ampere noncontinuous load is located 390 feet from a panelboard. What MINIMUM size THWN aluminum feeder conductors are required to limit the voltage drop to 3 percent? (K = 21.2)

A. 2 AWG
B. 1 AWG
C. 1/0 AWG
D. 2/0 AWG

END OF EXAM #14

TEXAS ELECTRICIANS PRACTICE EXAMS
MASTER ELECTRICIAN
EXAM #15

This is an "open book" practice exam. A calculator and a 2017 edition of the NATIONAL ELECTRICAL CODE® is the only reference that should be used. This exam is typical of questions that may be encountered on the Texas Master Electrician licensing exams. Select the best answer from the choices given and review your answers with the answer key included in this book.

ALLOTTED TIME: 75 minutes

1. Given: In a retail department store you are to install 100 feet of fixed multioutlet assembly where the cord-and-plug connected appliances are likely to be used simultaneously. What is the MINIMUM number of 120-volt, single-phase, 20 ampere branch-circuits required for this installation?

A. two
B. four
C. seven
D. eight

2. For a new recreational vehicle park, electrical services and feeders shall be calculated on the basis of NOT less than _____ per RV site equipped with 50-ampere, 208Y/120 or 120/240-volt supply facilities.

A. 9,600 VA
B. 12,000 VA
C. 3,600 VA
D. 7,200 VA

3. A twenty-five (25) ft. long tap conductor tapped from a 100 ampere rated feeder conductor, shall have an ampacity of NOT less than _____.

A. 50 amperes
B. 75 amperes
C. 25 amperes
D. 33.3 amperes

Copyright © 2017

4. In regard to electrified truck parking spaces in a truck plaza, upon loss of power from the local utility company or other electric supply systems, means shall be provided where energy ____.

A. can be fed with an ungrounded receptacle
B. cannot be fed with a portable generator
C. can be fed with a portable generator
D. cannot be back-fed through the truck and the truck supply equipment

5. Determine the demand load, in VA, on the ungrounded service-entrance conductors, for the general-lighting and receptacles for a 25,000 sq. ft. office building that has one hundred-fifty (150) general-purpose duplex receptacles. Consider the service overcurrent protection device is NOT listed for continuous use.

A. 112,075 VA
B. 106,000 VA
C. 90,200 VA
D. 127,875 VA

6. When an electrical service is required to have a grounded conductor present, what is the smallest grounded conductor permitted for an electric service using size 1000 kcmil copper ungrounded (phase) conductors?

A. 3/0 AWG copper
B. 2/0 AWG copper
C. 1/0 AWG copper
D. 4/0 AWG copper

7. Determine the MINIMUM number of 20-ampere, 277-volt, general-lighting branch circuits required for a 150,000 sq. ft. department store where the actual connected lighting load is 400 kVA.

A. 72 branch circuits
B. 82 branch circuits
C. 91 branch circuits
D. 102 branch circuits

8. Where a two-gang box contains two (2) single-pole switches, unless the box is equipped with permanently installed barriers, the voltage between the switches shall NOT be in excess of _____.

A. 120 volts
B. 277 volts
C. 240 volts
D. 300 volts

9. Disregarding exceptions, bonding between Class I, Divisions I and II locations and the point of grounding for service equipment shall be done by _____, regardless of the voltage of the electrical system wiring and equipment.

A. metal raceways
B. bonding jumpers
C. double locknuts
D. double locknuts and a metallic bushing

10. Shore power for boats docked in marinas and boatyards shall be provided by single receptacles that are of the locking and grounding type, mounted at least 12 inches above the deck surface, and rated NOT less than _____.

A. 50 amperes
B. 40 amperes
C. 30 amperes
D. 20 amperes

11. When rigid polyvinyl chloride conduit (PVC) is used to enclose conductors feeding a wet-niche luminaire in a permanently installed swimming pool, a _____ insulated copper grounding conductor shall be installed in this conduit, unless a listed low-voltage lighting system not requiring grounding is used.

A. 12 AWG
B. 10 AWG
C. 8 AWG
D. 6 AWG

12. When exceptions are not a consideration, what is the largest size dry-type transformer, in kVA, that may be installed in an area or room that is NOT constructed in a fire-resistant manner?

A. 75 KVA
B. 112½ KVA
C. 150 KVA
D. 50 KVA

13. For field wiring connections, NPT threaded entries into explosionproof equipment shall be made up with at LEAST _____ threads fully engaged.

A. four
B. five
C. three
D. six

14. An enclosure constructed so that moisture will not enter the enclosure under specified test conditions is regarded to as _____ in the NEC®.

A. weatherproof
B. watertight
C. raintight
D. weather-resistant

15. Conductors other than service-entrance conductors shall be permitted to be installed in a cable tray with service-entrance conductors provided _____.

A. a solid fixed barrier of material compatible with the cable tray is installed to separate the systems
B. the conductors are not in excess of 480 volts to ground
C. the voltage between the conductors is not in excess of 600 volts
D. the conductors have equal insulation and temperature ratings

16. The allowable ampacity of a size 750 kcmil XHHW aluminum conductor where there are six (6) current-carrying conductors in the raceway, installed in a dry location, where the ambient temperature will reach 22 deg. C is _____ .

A. 323.40 amperes
B. 365.40 amperes
C. 361.92 amperes
D. 348.00 amperes

Copyright © 2017

17. For the purposes of selecting the rating of the disconnecting means and controller for an ac motor, the locked-rotor current of a single-phase, one hp, 115-volt, ac motor is _____.

A. 16 amperes
B. 20 amperes
C. 48 amperes
D. 96 amperes

18. What is the MINIMUM size copper common grounding electrode conductor required to run through a building to four (4) separately derived systems (transformers) each having size 3/0 AWG copper secondary conductors?

A. 4 AWG
B. 2 AWG
C. 3/0 AWG
D. 8 AWG

19. Where a commercial building has a 600 ampere, 3-phase, 208Y/120 volt service supplied with two (2) paralled sets of size 350 kcmil copper conductors installed in separate raceways, determine the MINIMUM size aluminum grounding electrode conductor permitted to the metal water piping system used as the grounding electrode.
Assume the metal water piping system extends on to other types of electrodes.

A. 250 kcmil
B. 4/0 AWG
C. 3/0 AWG
D. 2/0 AWG

20. The NEC permits trade size 3/8 in. flexible metal conduit (FMC) to be used to enclose tap conductors for luminaires, provided the length of the FMC does NOT exceed _____.

A. 4 feet
B. 6 feet
C. 8 feet
D. 10 feet

21. What is the MAXIMUM distance allowed to support intermediate metal conduit (IMC) from a junction box, where structural members do not readily permit fastening?

A. 3 feet
B. 5 feet
C. 6 feet
D. 8 feet

22. Each operating room in a hospital shall be provided with a MINIMUM of _____ "hospital grade" receptacles divided between at least two branch circuits.

A. 8
B. 12
C. 24
D. 36

23. When combination surface nonmetallic raceways are used both for signaling and for power and lighting circuits, the different systems shall be _____.

A. prohibited
B. run in the same compartment
C. separated by at least ½ in.
D. run in separate compartments

24. When sizing fuses for a branch circuit serving a hermetic refrigerant motor-compressor, the device shall NOT exceed _____ of the rated load current marked on the nameplate of the equipment.

A. 115 percent
B. 125 percent
C. 175 percent
D. 225 percent

25. Explosionproof apparatus is required for equipment located in _____ locations.

A. Class I, Division 1 and 2
B. Class I, Division 3
C. Class II, Division 1 and 2
D. all of these

END OF EXAM #15

Copyright © 2017

TEXAS ELECTRICIANS PRACTICE EXAMS
MASTER ELECTRICIAN
EXAM #16

This is an "open book" practice exam. A calculator and a 2017 edition of the NATIONAL ELECTRICAL CODE® is the only reference that should be used. This exam is typical of questions that may be encountered on the Texas Master Electrician licensing exams. Select the best answer from the choices given and review your answers with the answer key in included in this book.

ALLOTTED TIME: 75 minutes

1. Exposed cables or raceways installed as part of an emergency system shall be permanently marked to be identified as a component of an emergency circuit or system at intervals NOT to exceed _____, where boxes or enclosures are not encountered.

A. 10 feet
B. 20 feet
C. 25 feet
D. 30 feet

2. Communications wires and cables shall have a voltage rating of NOT less than _____.

A. 60 volts
B. 120 volts
C. 300 volts
D. 600 volts

3. An emergency system is required to have NO more than _____ to have power available in the event of failure of the normal electrical supply system.

A. 10 seconds
B. 15 seconds
C. 45 seconds
D. 5 minutes

Copyright © 2017

4. X-ray equipment installed in a hospital may be served by a hard service cord with a suitable plug provided the branch-circuit rating does NOT exceed _____.

A. 15 amperes
B. 20 amperes
C. 30 amperes
D. 50 amperes

5. All metallic switchgear rated for over 1000 volts shall be provided with a grounding busbar, grounding conductor, or a grounding electrode for the purpose of connecting the _____.

A. grounded conductors
B. metallic shield of cables
C. metal raceways
D. ungrounded conductors

6. Given: A straight pull of size 4 AWG and larger conductors is to be made in a junction box that will have a trade size 3 in. conduit and two (2) trade size 2 in. conduits entering on the same side and exiting on the opposite wall. No splices will be contained in the box. Which of the following listed junction boxes is the MINIMUM required for this installation?

A. 18 in. x 12 in.
B. 20 in. x 18 in.
C. 24 in. x 24 in.
D. 30 in. x 30 in.

7. When wiring gasoline fuel dispensing pumps, the first fitting that should be installed in the raceway that emerges from below ground or concrete into the base of the fuel dispensers is a/an _____.

A. automatic cut-off breakaway valve
B. disconnecting means
C. sealing fitting
D. flexible fitting to prevent vibration

8. Determine the MAXIMUM overcurrent protection permitted for size 14 AWG THWN copper motor control-circuit conductors tapped from the load side of a motor overcurrent protection device. Given: The conductors require short-circuit protection and do not extend beyond the motor control equipment enclosure.

A. 20 amperes
B. 25 amperes
C. 30 amperes
D. 100 amperes

9. Where size 6 AWG THWN copper branch-circuit conductors supply a 240-volt, single-phase, 5,000 VA non-motor operated appliance, the MAXIMUM standard size circuit breaker permitted for overcurrent protection on this circuit is rated _____.

A. 55 amperes
B. 40 amperes
C. 35 amperes
D. 30 amperes

10. The ampacity of size 1/0 AWG THWN/THHN, dual-rated copper conductors enclosed in rigid metal conduit (RMC) when installed underground in direct contact with the earth is _____.

A. 170 amperes
B. 125 amperes
C. 130 amperes
D. 150 amperes

11. Electrical equipment such as switchboards, panelboards, industrial control panels, and motor control centers, located in commercial and industrial occupancies are required to be field marked to warn _____ of potential arc-flash hazards.

A. qualified persons
B. all personnel
C. unqualified persons
D. the authority having jurisdiction

12. Flexible metallic tubing (FMT) shall NOT be used in lengths over _____.

A. 5 feet
B. 6 feet
C. 8 feet
D. 10 feet

13. Battery back-up luminaires (unit equipment), provided for emergency illumination, such as in corridors of a school building, are to be permanently fixed in place, however they are permitted to be cord-and-plug connected provided the flexible cord does NOT exceed _____ in length.

A. 3 feet
B. 4 feet
C. 2 feet
D. 2 ½ feet

14. Determine the MAXIMUM permitted operational setting of an adjustable inverse time circuit breaker used for branch-circuit, short-circuit and ground-fault protection of a 15 hp, 208-volt, three-phase, squirrel cage, Design B, continuous-duty ac motor. Assume the rating you select will be sufficient for the starting current of the motor and exceptions need not be applied.

A. 46.20 amperes
B. 80.85 amperes
C. 115.5 amperes
D. 369.6 amperes

15. Every circuit breaker having an interrupting rating other than _____ shall have its interrupting rating shown on the circuit breaker.

A. 1,000 amperes
B. 10,000 amperes
C. 15,000 amperes
D. 5,000 amperes

16. Unless approved for a higher voltage, surface nonmetallic raceways are NOT permitted where the voltage is _____ or more between conductors.

A. 120 volts
B. 150 volts
C. 300 volts
D. 277 volts

17. Determine the MAXIMUM size overload protection required for a 480-volt, 3-phase, 15 hp, continuous-duty ac motor, where given the following related information. Assume the value you select will permit the overload device to carry the motor load and modification of this value is not required.

* Design C
* temperature rise - 40 deg. C
* service factor - 1.12
* nameplate ampere rating - 18 amperes

A. 20.7 amperes
B. 18.0 amperes
C. 22.5 amperes
D. 23.4 amperes

18. Any pipe or duct system foreign to the electrical installation must not enter a transformer vault. Which of the following listed is NOT considered foreign to the vault?

A. a roof drain
B. a building water main
C. an air duct passing through the vault
D. an automatic fire protection water sprinkler

19. Given: A 50 kVA transformer with a 480-volt, 3-phase, primary and a 208Y/120 volt, 3-phase secondary is to be installed. Overcurrent protection is required on both primary and secondary side of the transformer. Determine the MAXIMUM size overcurrent protection device permitted on the primary side.

A. 125 amperes
B. 150 amperes
C. 175 amperes
D. 200 amperes

20. In Class II, Division 1 locations, where pendant mounted luminaires are suspended by rigid metal conduit (RMC) and a means for flexibility is not provided, the RMC stem shall have a length of NOT more than _____.

A. 12 inches
B. 18 inches
C. 24 inches
D. 8 inches

Copyright © 2017

21. Where trade size ¾ in. flexible metallic tubing (FMT) may be infrequently flexed in service after installation, the radius of the bend shall NOT be less than _____.

A. 10 inches
B. 12 inches
C. 12½ inches
D. 17½ inches

22. A fifteen (15) ft. horizontal run of rigid metal conduit (RMC) is to be installed between two enclosures located in a Class II, Division 1 hazardous location. One enclosure is dust ignitionproof, the other is not. The NEC® requires a MINIMUM of _____ sealing fittings.

A. none required
B. one
C. two
D. three

23. Where conduits or other raceways enter floor-standing switchboards, panelboards, or switchgear from the bottom, the conduits or raceways, including their end fittings, shall NOT rise more than _____ above the bottom of the enclosure.

A. 4 inches
B. 6 inches
C. 2 inches
D. 3 inches

24. When sizing pull and junction boxes for use on electrical systems over 1000 volts, for straight pulls, the length of the box shall NOT be less than _____ the outside diameter of the outer sheath of the largest shielded or lead-covered conductor or cable entering the box.

A. 48 times
B. 36 times
C. 32 times
D. 24 times

25. As a general rule, direct-buried cables of 13,000 volts must be buried at a depth of NOT less than _____.

A. 24 inches
B. 30 inches
C. 36 inches
D. 42 inches

END OF EXAM #16

TEXAS ELECTRICIANS PRACTICE EXAMS
SIGN ELECTRICIAN
EXAM #17

This is an "open book" practice exam. A calculator and a 2017 edition of the NATIONAL ELECTRICAL CODE® is the only reference that should be used. This exam is typical of questions that may be encountered on the Texas Journeyman and Master Sign Electricians licensing exams. Select the best answer from the choices given and review your answers with the answer key included in this book.

ALLOTTED TIME: 75 minutes

1. Which of the following conductor insulation types listed is NOT suitable for use in rigid polyvinyl chloride conduit (PVC), where buried underground in direct contact with the earth?

A. TW
B. THHN
C. THWN
D. XHHW

2. Neon tubing shall be supported by listed tube supports. The neon tubing shall be supported within _____ from the electrode connection.

A. 6 inches
B. 8 inches
C. 10 inches
D. 12 inches

3. In regard to a neon sign, switches controlling transformers and electric power supplies shall be rated for controlling inductive loads or have a current rating of _____, where the current rating of a neon sign transformer is 10 amperes.

A. 10 amperes
B. 15 amperes
C. 25 amperes
D. 20 amperes

Copyright © 2017

4. Where a 20-ampere, 120-volt, single-phase, branch circuit is to supply an electric sign, what is the MAXIMUM voltage drop the NEC® recommends on this branch circuit?

A. 2.4 volts
B. 3.6 volts
C. 5.0 volts
D. 6.0 volts

5. A fixed or stationary electric sign installed inside a decorative fountain shall be at LEAST _____ inside the fountain, when measured from the outside edges of the fountain.

A. 3 feet
B. 5 feet
C. 6 feet
D. 10 feet

6. Portable or mobile electric signs placed in wet or damp locations shall be _____ .

   I. provided with factory-installed GFCI protection
   II. listed

A. I only
B. II only
C. both I and II
D. neither I nor II

7. When installing buried underground rigid metal conduit (RMC) under a parking lot of a retail outlet mall to supply an electric sign, the MINIMUM burial depth of the RMC is _____ .

A. 6 inches
B. 12 inches
C. 18 inches
D. 24 inches

Copyright © 2017

8. The National Electrical Code® requires equipment grounding conductors to be _____.

   I. green in color or bare
   II. white or gray in color

A. I only
B. II only
C. either I or II
D. neither I nor II

9. Which of the following is NOT required to be marked on an electric sign?

A. manufacturer's name
B. input voltage
C. current rating
D. serial number

10. What is the MINIMUM size conductor permitted for wiring neon secondary circuits rated at 1,000 volts or less?

A. 14 AWG
B. 12 AWG
C. 16 AWG
D. 18 AWG

11. The MAXIMUM number of size 8 AWG THW conductors permitted to be installed in an electrical trade size 3/4 in. Schedule 40 rigid PVC conduit is _____.

A. three
B. four
C. five
D. six

12. Where an electric sign is installed within a fountain or within 10 ft. of the fountain edge, the sign shall be provided with a local, within sight, readily accessible, disconnecting means located at NOT less than _____ horizontally from the inside walls of the fountain, unless separated from the open water by a permanent barrier.

A. 5 feet
B. 10 feet
C. 20 feet
D. 25 feet

Copyright © 2017

13. A portable electric sign shall not be placed within a pool or fountain or within _____ from the inside walls of the pool or fountain.

A. 5 feet
B. 10 feet
C. 15 feet
D. 20 feet

14. Where an electric sign is to be installed in the parking lot of a retail store and is not provided with barriers to protect it from physical damage; the sign is required to be at LEAST _____ above the areas accessible to vehicular traffic.

A. 10 feet
B. 12 feet
C. 14 feet
D. 16 feet

15. For other than neon tubing installations, branch circuits that supply outline lighting systems shall be rated NOT to exceed _____.

A. 15 amperes
B. 20 amperes
C. 30 amperes
D. 40 amperes

16. Which of the following listed types of connector is prohibited for connection of a grounding conductor to equipment?

A. solder
B. pressure connectors
C. clamps
D. lugs

17. Given: An electrical service for a highway billboard electric sign consisting of three (3), 2-wire branch circuits is to be installed. The service disconnecting means shall have a rating of at LEAST _____.

A. 15 amperes
B. 30 amperes
C. 60 amperes
D. 100 amperes

Copyright © 2017

18. Branch circuit conductors within 3 inches of a ballast or transformer of a luminaire (lighting fixture) shall have a temperature rating of NOT less than _____.

A. 105°C
B. 90°C
C. 75°C
D. 60°C

19. Branch circuits or feeders supplying electric signs installed within a fountain or within at LEAST _____ of the fountain edge shall have ground-fault protection for personnel.

A. 10 feet
B. 20 feet
C. 25 feet
D. 30 feet

20. Where a 12 ft. nonmetallic pole is used to support an electric sign which is used as a raceway, which of the following is required?

A. The conductors must be in a multiconductor cable.
B. The pole must be metallic, nonmetallic poles are prohibited to support electric signs.
C. A handhole cover that is suitable for wet locations must be provided.
D. All of these are required.

21. For the purpose of calculations, branch circuits that supply electric sign loads are to be considered _____ loads.

A. intermittent
B. noncontinuous
C. short-time
D. continuous

22. Branch circuit conductors supplying outdoor placed incandescent and fluorescent lighted electric signs shall have a voltage of NOT more than _____ to ground.

A. 277 volts
B. 250 volts
C. 120 volts
D. 480 volts

23. The MAXIMUM allowable ampacity of size 8 AWG THWN copper conductors installed in a 100 ft. length of conduit is _____, when there are not more than three (3) current-carrying conductors in the conduit and ambient temperature is not a factor.

A. 40 amperes
B. 50 amperes
C. 55 amperes
D. 65 amperes

24. Each commercial building accessible to pedestrians shall have an outside sign circuit rated at LEAST _____ that supplies no other load.

A. 15 amperes
B. 20 amperes
C. 25 amperes
D. 30 amperes

25. As a general rule, each electric sign is to be provided with a disconnect intended to allow service or maintenance personnel complete and local control of the disconnecting means. The required disconnect may be located _____.

I. at the point the circuit conductors supplying the sign enters a sign enclosure or a pole
II. at any distance, if within sight of the sign
III. out of sight of the sign, if with 75 feet of the sign

A. I only
B. II only
C. either I or II
D. either I, II, or III

END OF EXAM #17

Copyright © 2017

TEXAS ELECTRICIANS PRACTICE EXAMS
SIGN ELECTRICIAN
EXAM #18

This is an "open book" practice exam. A calculator and a 2017 edition of the NATIONAL ELECTRICAL CODE® is the only reference that should be used. This exam is typical of questions that may be encountered on the Texas Journeyman and Master Sign Electricians licensing exams. Select the best answer from the choices given and review your answers with the answer key included in this book.

ALLOTTED TIME: 75 minutes

1. Given: You are to install a transformer in an attic of a department store and the transformer serves an electric sign installed outdoors in the front of the building. This installation is permitted, if there is an access door of at LEAST ____ to the transformer.

A. 24 in. x 22½ in.
B. 36 in. x 22½ in.
C. 36 in. x 30 in.
D. 48 in. x 32 in.

2. Where field-installed skeleton tubing installations consists of splices in systems over 1,000 volts, conductor splices shall be ____ rated over 1,000 volts.

A. on open insulators
B. made in listed enclosures
C. made by pressure connectors
D. connected to a conductor with insulation

3. What is the MINIMUM number of 125-volt, 15- or 20-ampere single-phase, receptacle outlets the NEC® mandates to be installed on an electric sign?

A. none
B. one
C. two
D. three

4. Where direct-buried cable is the wiring method used to supply an outdoor electric sign, which of the following listed cables is approved for such use?

Copyright © 2017

A. Type NMB
B. Type NMDB
C. Type UF
D. All of these are approved for direct burial.

5. A MINIMUM spacing of NOT less than _____ shall be maintained between neon tubing and any surface, other than its support.

A. 1/4 inches
B. 3/8 inches
C. 1/2 inches
D. 5/8 inches

6. Luminaires located in an electric sign shall be installed so that adjacent combustible materials will not be subject to temperatures in excess of _____.

A. 30°C
B. 60°C
C. 75°C
D. 90°C

7. Direct-buried cables that emerge from grade and up a pole must be installed in an enclosure or raceway in order to be protected from physical damage, and protection above finished grade must extend to a height of NOT less than _____.

A. 6 feet
B. 8 feet
C. 18 inches
D. 6 ½ feet

8. What is the MAXIMUM length allowed for cords supplying portable or mobile signs placed in dry locations?

A. 10 feet
B. 6 feet
C. 15 feet
D. 25 feet

9. The overcurrent protection for size 10 AWG copper branch-circuit conductors serving a HID lighted sign shall NOT exceed _____.

A. 15 amperes
B. 20 amperes
C. 25 amperes
D. 30 amperes

10. Bonding conductors provided for electric signs shall be sized at NOT less than size _____ copper.

A. 14 AWG
B. 12 AWG
C. 10 AWG
D. 8 AWG

11. Ballasts and transformers installed in an attic above suspended ceilings shall NOT be connected to the branch circuit by _____.

A. flexible metal conduit (FMC)
B. armored cable (AC)
C. electrical nonmetallic tubing (ENT)
D. flexible cord

12. An unbroken length of rigid metal conduit (RMC) or intermediate meatal conduit (IMC) shall be permitted to support a luminaire installed for a billboard sign in lieu of a box if which of the following rule is met?

A. The luminaire may be installed 12 ft. above grade if the billboard is not accessible to unqualified persons.
B. The length of conduit exceeds 4 ft. from the last point of conduit support.
C. The luminaire is 15 inches in any direction from any single conduit entry.
D. The total supported weight on a single conduit exceeds 20 pounds.

13. The proper term for a conductor used to ground an electric motor in a sign is the _____ conductor.

A. ground
B. neutral
C. grounded
D. equipment grounding

14. What is the MAXIMUM number of 90 deg. bends permitted in a run of rigid nonmetallic conduit (PVC) to serve a sign if there are no junction boxes provided?

A. two
B. three
C. four
D. six

15. When a commercial building accessible to pedestrians has a branch circuit that is supplying a sign that contains neon tubing installations only, the branch circuit shall be rated at a MAXIMUM value of _____.

A. 15 amperes
B. 20 amperes
C. 30 amperes
D. 40 amperes

16. The NEC® requires locations of lamps for outdoor lighting to be below all energized conductors or other electric utilization equipment; an exception to this requirement would be which of the following?

A. The lamps shall be within 6½ feet of the ground level.
B. A lockable disconnecting means must be provided.
C. Conductors are to be identified by orange insulation.
D. The lamps must have an isolated grounding conductor.

17. Disregarding exceptions, when sign enclosures are supported by metal poles and the poles contain supply conductors to the sign, a handhole of NOT less than _____ is required at the base of the pole to provide access to the supply terminations.

A. 2 in. x 4 in.
B. 4 in. x 4 in.
C. 4 in. x 6 in.
D. 6 in. x 6 in.

Copyright © 2017

18. What is the MAXIMUM length permitted for flexible metal conduit (FMC) where used as a bonding means, when the flex encloses secondary conductors from a transformer for use with neon tubing?

A. 6 feet
B. 10 feet
C. 20 feet
D. 100 feet

19. Due to expansion, what change in length will a 200 feet run of Schedule 40 PVC conduit have, where the PVC conduit is installed outdoors and is exposed to an annual 90°F temperature variation from the warmest day to the coldest day?

A. 3.65 inches
B. 7.30 inches
C. 10.96 inches
D. 3.75 inches

20. All motors installed on signs shall be considered as _____, unless the nature of the apparatus it drives is such that the motor will not operate continuously.

A. periodic duty
B. short-time duty
C. intermittent duty
D. continuous duty

21. Determine the MINIMUM electrical trade size intermediate metal conduit (IMC) permitted by the NEC® to enclose three (3) size 8 AWG THHW and one (1) size 10 AWG THHW copper conductors in a 75 ft. conduit run.

A. 1/2 in.
B. 3/4 in.
C. 1 in.
D. 1¼ in.

22. For field installed neon secondary circuits over 1,000 volts, the length of the secondary circuit conductors from the transformer leads to the first neon tube electrode shall NOT exceed _____ where installed in metal conduit or tubing.

A. 10 feet
B. 20 feet
C. 50 feet
D. 100 feet

23. An electrical device used to reduce voltage without changing the available power is a/an _____.

A. rectifier
B. amplifier
C. transformer
D. capacitor

24. What is the MINIMUM size copper conductors required for an overhead span when serving a pole-mounted electric sign that has a total load of 1,800 VA, where given the following related information?

* 120 volt, single-phase source
* 25 feet between supports
* no messenger wire is provided

A. 8 AWG
B. 10 AWG
C. 12 AWG
D. 14 AWG

25. Given: A pole-mounted electric sign is to be installed at a convenience store with gasoline and diesel motor fuel dispensing units. The sign is to be supplied by branch circuit conductors installed in buried rigid polyvinyl chloride conduit (PVC). In order for the PVC to be outside of the area classified as a hazardous location, the conduit is required to be at LEAST _____ from the motor fuel dispensing units.

A. 21 feet
B. 25 feet
C. 30 feet
D. 50 feet

END OF EXAM #18

Copyright © 2017

Final Exams

Copyright © 2017

TEXAS ELECTRICIANS PRACTICE EXAMS
RESIDENTIAL ELECTRICANS FINAL EXAM

This is an "open book" practice exam. A calculator and a 2017 edition of the NATIONAL ELECTRICAL CODE® is the only reference that should be used. This exam is typical of questions that may be encountered on the Texas Residential Wireman licensing exams. Select the best answer from the choices given and review your answers with the answer key included in this book. Passing score on this practice exam is 75%. The exam consists of 60 questions valued at 1.66 points each, so you must answer at least 45 questions correct for a passing score. If you do not score at least 75%, try again and keep studying.

ALLOTTED TIME: 3 hours

1. Conductors tapped from a 50 ampere branch circuit supplying electric ranges, wall-mounted electric ovens and counter-mounted cooktops must have an ampacity of at LEAST _____ and be of sufficient size for the load.

A. 15 amperes
B. 20 amperes
C. 30 amperes
D. 40 amperes

2. All 120-volt, single-phase, 15- and 20-ampere outlets that supply built-in dishwashers installed in dwelling unit kitchens shall be provided with _____.

   I. GFCI protection
   II. AFCI protection

A. I only
B. II only
C. both I and II
D. neither I nor II

3. The ampacity of the branch-circuit conductors that supply a residential fixed storage-type electric water heater of 120 gallons or less, shall have a rating of NOT less than _____ of the marked nameplate rating of the water heater.

A. 80 percent
B. 100 percent
C. 125 percent
D. 150 percent

Copyright © 2017

4. Given: A 240-volt, single-phase, 16.8 kW, household electric range is to be installed in a one-family dwelling. Determine the MINIMUM size copper Type NM cable required for branch-circuit conductors to supply the range.

A. 8 AWG
B. 6 AWG
C. 4 AWG
D. 2 AWG

5. The service equipment for an individual mobile home shall have a rating of NOT less than _____ at 120/240-volts, single-phase.

A. 100 amperes
B. 60 amperes
C. 125 amperes
D. 150 amperes

6. The ampacity of Types NM, NMC and NMS cable shall be in accordance with the _____ conductor temperature rating, and the _____ rating shall be permitted to be used for ampacity adjustment and correction calculations.

A. 60 deg. C - 75 deg. C
B. 60 deg. C - 90 deg. C
C. 75 deg. C - 90 deg. C
D. 60 deg. C - 90 deg. F

7. For dwelling units, receptacle outlets shall be installed so that no point along the wall line of a kitchen countertop or work surface is more than _____, measured horizontally, from a receptacle outlet in that space.

A. 12 inches
B. 16 inches
C. 18 inches
D. 24 inches

8. For the purpose of determining conductor fill in a device box, the NEC® mandates a switch to be counted as equal to two (2) conductors. The volume allowance for the two (2) conductors shall be based on:

A. the largest wire in the box.
B. the largest grounding conductor in the box.
C. the largest wire connected to the switch.
D. the number of clamps in the box.

9. A point in the wiring system at which current is taken to supply utilization equipment, is defined as a/an ____ .

A. receptacle
B. branch-circuit
C. junction box
D. outlet

10. Bends in Type NM cable shall be made so that the radius of the curve of the inner edge of any bend shall NOT be less than:

A. five times the diameter of the cable.
B. seven times the diameter of the cable.
C. seven times the circular mil area of the conductors.
D. five times the circular mil area of the conductors.

11. For residential electric ranges rated at 8.75 kW or more, the MINIMUM branch circuit rating shall be ____ .

A. 30 amperes
B. 40 amperes
C. 50 amperes
D. 60 amperes

12. In walls or ceilings with a surface of concrete, tile, gypsum, plaster or other noncombustible material, boxes employing a flush-type cover or faceplate shall be installed so that the front edge of the box will NOT set back of the finished surface
more than _____ .

A. 1/4 in.
B. 1/2 in.
C. 3/8 in.
D. 3/4 in.

Copyright © 2017

13. Switching devices must be located at LEAST _____ from the inside walls of a permanently installed swimming pool, unless separated from the pool by a solid fence, wall or other permanent barrier.

A. 5 feet
B. 10 feet
C. 15 feet
D. 20 feet

14. All 125-volt, single-phase, 15- and 20-ampere receptacle outlets installed in the following locations of dwelling units, shall be protected by a listed ground-fault circuit interrupter EXCEPT _____.

A. garages
B. bathrooms
C. hallways
D. outdoors

15. Where a 20-ampere rated branch circuit supplies multiple residential kitchen countertop or work surface outlets, the receptacle outlets shall have a rating of _____.

A. 20 amperes only
B. 15 or 20 amperes
C. 10, 15 or 20 amperes
D. 15 amperes only

16. Determine the allowable ampacity of a size 12/2 with ground Type NMC copper cable when installed in an area where the ambient temperature reaches 103 deg. F and the cable is bundled for 6 feet with three (3) other 120 volt circuits using the same cable.

A. 21.8 amperes
B. 15.26 amperes
C. 19.11 amperes
D. 18.2 amperes

17. Underground service conductors that are not encased in concrete and buried 18 inches or more below grade shall have their location identified by a warning ribbon that is placed in the trench at LEAST _____ above the underground installation.

A. 6 inches
B. 12 inches
C. 18 inches
D. 24 inches

18. When the white colored insulated conductor in a NM cable is used for a three-way switch loop, the conductor shall be _____.

A. permanently reidentified with green colored tape
B. a return conductor only
C. used only for the supply to the switch
D. a grounding conductor only

19. Where a mobile home has the main service disconnecting means installed outdoors, the disconnecting means shall be installed so the bottom of the enclosure is NOT less than _____ above finished grade.

A. one foot
B. two feet
C. three feet
D. four feet

20. In general, with respect to the service disconnecting means, a grounding connection shall be made to the grounded conductor on _____.

 I. the supply side
 II. the load side

A. I only
B. II only
C. both I and II
D. neither I nor II

Copyright © 2017

21. When installed in dwelling unit bedrooms, which of the following listed is/are required to be protected by an AFCI protection device?

A. receptacles
B. lighting fixtures
C. ceiling fans
D. all of these

22. Mandatory rules of the NEC® are those that identify actions that are specifically required or prohibited are characterized by the use of the terms _____.

A. shall or shall not
B. may or may not
C. will or will not
D. can or cannot

23. The service disconnecting means for a dwelling unit shall consist of NOT more than _____ switches or circuit breakers.

A. one
B. two
C. six
D. eight

24. Where nonmetallic sheathed cable (NM) is used with nonmetallic boxes no larger than 2¼ in. x 4 in., the cable is not required to be secured to the box where the cable is fastened within at LEAST _____ of the box.

A. 6 inches
B. 8 inches
C. 12 inches
D. 10 inches

25. A receptacle that provides power to a swimming pool recirculating water-pump motor, shall be permitted NOT less than _____ from the inside wall of the pool and shall have GFCI protection.

A. 5 feet
B. 6 feet
C. 8 feet
D. 10 feet

Copyright © 2017

26. Conductor insulation shall be rated at _____ for Types NM, NMC and NM-B cable.

A. 60 deg. C
B. 75 deg. C
C. 90 deg. C
D. 90 deg. F

27. Given: A direct-buried landscape lighting branch circuit carries 24 volts and uses Type UF cable as the wiring method. This cable must be buried with an earth cover of at LEAST _____, where the cable does not cross under the driveway, alley or the street.

A. 6 inches
B. 12 inches
C. 18 inches
D. 24 inches

28. In a dwelling unit bedroom, any wall space that is at LEAST _____ or more in width must be provided with a general-use receptacle outlet.

A. 2 feet
B. 4 feet
C. 6 feet
D. 10 feet

29. Edison base plug fuses are permitted only for _____.

A. new work
B. replacement
C. motor circuits
D. lighting circuits

30. A cord-and-attachment plug-connected room air conditioner shall NOT exceed _____ of the rating of the branch circuit where no other loads are supplied.

A. 80 percent
B. 75 percent
C. 60 percent
D. 50 percent

31. Track lighting or ceiling-suspended (paddle) fans are not to be located less than _____ horizontally from the top of the bathtub rim or shower stall threshold.

A. 6 feet
B. 8 feet
C. 4 feet
D. 3 feet

32. A 125-volt, single-phase, 15- or 20- ampere rated receptacle outlet shall be installed at each residential kitchen countertop space and work surface space that is at LEAST _____ or wider.

A. 48 inches
B. 36 inches
C. 24 inches
D. 12 inches

33. What is the MAXIMUM length of a flexible cord that may be used for a recirculating water-pump motor provided for a permanently installed swimming pool at a dwelling?

A. 3 feet
B. 4 feet
C. 6 feet
D. 10 feet

34. A part of an electrical system that is intended to carry or control electric energy as its principal function is referred to as a _____.

A. device
B. fitting
C. raceway
D. enclosure

35. In dwelling unit bathrooms, at least one GFCI protected general-use receptacle outlet shall be installed at NOT more than _____ from of the outside edge of each basin.

A. 4 feet
B. 6 feet
C. 3 feet
D. 2 feet

36. Type UF cable is NOT permitted to be used _____.

Copyright © 2017

A. in an attic space
B. as service-entrance cable
C. as a substitute for NM cable
D. for solar photovoltaic systems

37. What is the MAXIMUM distance a 15- or 20-ampere, 125-volt, single-phase, receptacle may be installed from a hot tub installed outdoors at a dwelling unit?

A. 20 feet
B. 15 feet
C. 10 feet
D. 5 feet

38. In general, an equipment bonding jumper installed on the outside of a raceway may NOT exceed _____ in length.

A. 8 feet
B. 6 feet
C. 4 feet
D. 3 feet

39. Surface-mounted enclosed incandescent luminaires (lighting fixtures) are permitted to be installed on the wall or ceiling of a closet, provided there is a MINIMUM clearance of _____ between the luminaire and the nearest point of storage space.

A. 12 inches
B. 8 inches
C. 6 inches
D. 18 inches

40. Unless specifically permitted elsewhere in the NEC®, as a general rule, for size 10 AWG copper Type NM cable the overcurrent protection shall NOT exceed _____.

A. 25 amperes
B. 20 amperes
C. 35 amperes
D. 30 amperes

41. Using the standard (general) method of calculation for a one-family dwelling, determine the MINIMUM demand load, in VA, on the ungrounded service-entrance conductors when the house has the following fixed appliances:

   * water heater - 4800 VA
   * dishwasher - 1200 VA
   * garbage disposal - 1150 VA
   * trash compactor - 800 VA
   * attic fan - 1200 VA

A. 6,863 VA
B. 9,150 VA
C. 8,579 VA
D. 11,438 VA

42. Where a single-family dwelling having a computed load of 175 amperes is to be provided with a 120/240 volt service-drop from the local utility company, what is the MINIMUM size aluminum conductors with THWN insulation permitted for use as ungrounded service-entrance conductors for the house?

A. 1/0 AWG
B. 2/0 AWG
C. 3/0 AWG
D. 4/0 AWG

43. Where a 20-ampere rated branch circuit in a residence supplies only fixed resistance type baseboard heaters, the circuit may be loaded to a MAXIMUM value of _____.

A. 16 amperes
B. 20 amperes
C. 18 amperes
D. 14 amperes

44. When an evaporative cooler is mounted on the roof of a one-family dwelling, where is the service receptacle outlet to be located?

A. Within 75 ft. of the unit.
B. Within 50 ft. of the unit and on the same level.
C. Within 25 ft. of the unit and on the same level.
D. Not required for one-family dwelling units.

45. Disregarding exceptions, the MAXIMUM distance permitted for seven (7) current carrying NM cables to be bundled together without requiring the ampacity of the conductors to be adjusted is _____.

A. 4 feet
B. 12 inches
C. 18 inches
D. 24 inches

46. As a general rule, receptacle outlets provided for the small appliance countertop circuits in the kitchen of a dwelling, shall be located above the countertop and work surface, but NOT more than _____ above the countertop or work surface.

A. 8 inches
B. 12 inches
C. 20 inches
D. 18 inches

47. Unless otherwise permitted, the service grounding electrode conductor is sized in accordance with the rating of _____.

A. the main circuit breaker or disconnecting means
B. service-drop conductors
C. the service-entrance conductors
D. the ground rod

48. Which of the following is permitted to be connected to the 120-volt, 20-ampere branch circuit provided for the bathroom receptacle outlets in a dwelling?

A. GFCI protected receptacles in the garage
B. GFCI protected receptacles located outdoors
C. lighting outlets in the bathroom
D. Such circuits are not permitted to supply other outlets.

49. When wall-mounted, the required 125-volt, 15- and 20-ampere rated general-purpose receptacles in dwelling units, shall NOT be located more than _____ above the floor.

A. 5½ feet
B. 4 feet
C. 18 inches
D. 4½ feet

Copyright © 2017

50. Generally, where a 20- ampere rated branch circuit supplies a single receptacle, the receptacle must have an ampere rating of at LEAST _____.

A. 10 amperes
B. 15 amperes
C. 20 amperes
D. 16 amperes

51. Residential foyers that are not part of a hallway and that have an area that is at least GREATER than _____ shall have a receptacle(s) located in each wall space 3 feet or more in width.

A. 100 sq. ft.
B. 50 sq. ft.
C. 80 sq. ft.
D. 60 sq. ft.

52. Where installing a receptacle for a specific appliance such as an electric range, it must be placed within NO more than _____ of the intended location of the appliance.

A. 4 feet
B. 6 feet
C. 8 feet
D. 5 feet

53. What is the MINIMUM number of 120-volt, 15 ampere, single-phase, general lighting branch circuits required for a dwelling unit having a lighting load of 9,600 VA?

A. five
B. six
C. three
D. seven

54. In each hallway of a dwelling unit that is at LEAST _____ long, measured along the centerline, without passing through a doorway, at least one 125-volt, single-phase, 15- or 20- ampere, general-use receptacle must be installed.

A. 10 feet
B. 20 feet
C. 15 feet
D. 8 feet

55. When calculating the general lighting load for a dwelling unit, which of the following is NOT required to be included in the calculation?

A. bathrooms
B. closets
C. open porches
D. hallways

56. As stated in the NEC®, a luminaire that weighs more than _____ or exceeds 16 inches in any dimension shall not be supported by the screw shell of a lampholder.

A. 5 lbs.
B. 10 lbs.
C. 8 lbs.
D. 6 lbs.

57. For one-and two-family dwellings, solar photovoltaic system dc circuits shall be permitted to have a MAXIMUM voltage of _____ or less.

A. 30 volts
B. 48 volts
C. 120 volts
D. 600 volts

58. Electrical boxes installed in a kitchen countertop back-splash having a combustible finish shall be _____.

A. recessed ¼ in.
B. recessed a minimum of ½ in.
C. projected not less than 1¼ in.
D. flush or projected from the finish

59. Each dwelling unit is required to be provided with a MINIMUM of _____ small-appliance branch circuit(s).

A. one (1), 20-ampere
B. two (2), 20-ampere
C. two (2), 15-ampere
D. two (2), 15- or 20-ampere

60. The service equipment for a mobile home must be located within sight from and NOT more than _____ from the exterior wall of the mobile home it serves.

A. 100 feet
B. 50 feet
C. 30 feet
D. 25 feet

END OF RESIDENTIAL ELECTRICIANS FINAL EXAM

TEXAS ELECTRICIANS PRACTICE EXAMS
JOURNEYMAN ELECTRICIANS FINAL EXAM

This is an "open book" practice exam. A calculator and a 2017 edition of the NATIONAL ELECTRICAL CODE® is the only reference that should be used. This exam is typical of questions that may be encountered on the Texas Journeyman Electrician licensing exams. Select the best answer from the choices given and review your answers with the answer key included in this book. Passing score on this practice exam is 75%. The exam consists of 80 questions valued at 1.25 points each, so you must answer at least 60 questions correct for a passing score. If you do not score at least 75%, try again and keep studying.

ALLOTTED TIME: 4 hours

1. Where a building or structure is provided with a 3-phase, 480Y/277-volt service, each disconnecting means rated at LEAST _____ or more shall be provided with ground-fault protection.

A. 1000 amperes
B. 1200 amperes
C. 1500 amperes
D. 2000 amperes

2. What is the MINIMUM number of general-use receptacle outlets that must be located in a residential kitchen island countertop with a long dimension of 48 inches and 18 inches wide?

A. none
B. one
C. two
D. three

3. As a general rule, where a feeder supplies a continuous-load of 240 amperes the overcurrent protection device protecting this circuit shall have a rating of at LEAST _____.

A. 240 amperes
B. 200 amperes
C. 275 amperes
D. 300 amperes

4. The color coding permitted to identify intrinsically safe conductors is _____ and where no other conductors of the same color are used.

Copyright © 2017

A. light green
B. light blue
C. dark green
D. orange

5. When wiring gasoline motor fuel dispensing pumps, the first fitting that should be installed in the raceway that emerges from below ground or concrete into the base of the gasoline dispenser is a/an:

A. automatic cut-off breakaway valve.
B. disconnect.
C. sealing fitting.
D. no fittings of any kind are permitted in this location.

6. Overhead spans of open conductors of not over 300 volts to ground shall have a clearance of NOT less than _____ over residential driveways.

A. 10 feet
B. 12 feet
C. 15 feet
D. 18 feet

7. When sizing the overcurrent protection for a single non-motor operated appliance such as a storage-type water heater, cooktop or electric range, which of the following need NOT to be taken into consideration?

A. The length of time the appliance operates.
B. The full-load current marked on the appliance.
C. The voltage rating of the appliance
D. Where the overcurrent protection device selected is not a standard sixe.

8. The classification of hazardous areas and zones is to be determined by _____.

A. engineers
B. licensed electricians
C. qualified persons
D. the local authority having jurisdiction

Copyright © 2017

9. A metal junction box to be installed will contain the following:

   * three - 6 AWG conductors, 2 ungrounded & 1 grounded
   * one - 8 AWG equipment grounding conductor
   * two - internal clamps
   * one - pigtail

Determine the MINIMUM size box, in cubic inches, required.

A. 16 cubic inches
B. 18 cubic inches
C. 20 cubic inches
D. 23 cubic inches

10. Infrared lamp commercial and industrial heating appliances shall have overcurrent protection NOT exceeding _____.

A. 20 amperes
B. 40 amperes
C. 50 amperes
D. 60 amperes

11. For temporary wiring installations that have an assured equipment grounding conductor program, all required tests shall be performed at intervals NOT exceeding _____.

A. 3 months
B. 2 months
C. 6 months
D. 1 month

12. Which of the following circuits is prohibited for the grounded conductor to be dependent on receptacle devices for continuity?

A. All circuits.
B. Multi-outlet circuits.
C. GFCI protected circuits.
D. Multiwire circuits.

13. The lightning protections system ground terminals shall be bonded to _____.

A. the grounded terminal bar at the main disconnecting means
B. the ungrounded terminal bar at the main disconnecting means
C. the building or structure grounding electrode system
D. none of these, it shall be isolated from the building or structure

14. When a galvanized eye-bolt is to be used as the point of attachment for overhead electrical service conductors, the NEC® requires the eye-bolt to be installed NOT less than _____ above finished grade.

A. 8 feet
B. 12 feet
C. 10 feet
D. 15 feet

15. Under which one of the following conditions are you required to use an approved electrically conductive corrosion resistance compound on metal conduit threads?

A. In Class I Division 1 locations.
B. In Class II Division 1 locations.
C. On field cut threads for indoor locations.
D. On field cut threads in corrosive locations.

16. Disregarding exceptions, each patient bed location in critical (Category 1) spaces of hospitals shall be supplied by:

   I. one or more branch-circuits from the critical branch.
   II. one or more branch-circuits from the normal system.

A. I only
B. II only
C. either I or II
D. both I and II

17. Individual freestanding-type, cord-and-plug connected office furnishing partitions, shall NOT contain more than _____ 15-ampere, 125-volt duplex receptacle outlets.

A. six
B. thirteen
C. ten
D. eight

Copyright © 2017

18. Overhead service-drop conductors shall NOT be smaller than size _____, unless the service conductors supply only limited loads of a single branch circuit.

A. 8 AWG copper
B. 6 AWG copper
C. 8 AWG aluminum
D. 2 AWG aluminum

19. Given: A 5 hp, 208-volt, 3-phase squirrel-cage motor with no code letter is marked with a temperature rise of 40 deg. C and has a nameplate rating of 16 amperes. Where an adjustable overload device is used to protect the motor, this device shall be selected to trip at NO more than _____. Assume the value you select will be sufficient to carry the motor load and modification of this value is not necessary.

A. 18.4 amperes
B. 20.0 amperes
C. 22.4 amperes
D. 20.8 amperes

20. The short-circuit and ground-fault protective device protecting the motor-compressor branch circuit shall have sufficient _____ to permit the motor-compressor and other motors to start and accelerate their loads.

A. overcurrent protection
B. rating
C. time delay
D. both A and B

21. What MINIMUM size bonding conductor must bond all metal parts associated with an indoor installed hot tub?

A. 12 AWG
B. 10 AWG
C. 8 AWG
D. 6 AWG

22. Listed flexible metal conduit (FMC) is approved for use as an equipment grounding conductor where the FMC is not longer than 6 feet and the circuit conductors contained in the FMC are protected by overcurrent devices rated NOT more than _____.

A. 15 amperes
B. 20 amperes
C. 30 amperes
D. 40 amperes

23. An equipotential bonding grid must be installed in the deck around a permanently installed swimming pool; the bonding grid shall extend for at LEAST _____ horizontally beyond the inside walls of the pool.

A. 3 feet
B. 5 feet
C. 6 feet
D. 10 feet

24. For the purpose of calculating the general lighting load for a dwelling unit, the floor area should include all the following EXCEPT _____.

A. kitchens
B. bathrooms
C. an unfinished basement intended for future living space
D. an open porch not adaptable for future use

25. Where the outer sheath of Type MI cable is made of steel _____.

A. it shall provide an adequate path to serve as an equipment grounding conductor
B. a separate equipment grounding conductor shall be provided
C. the grounding and grounded conductors shall be bonded together
D. it shall not be longer than 6 feet

26. Motors shall be located so that adequate _____ is provided and so that maintenance, such as lubrication of bearings and replacing of brushes can be readily accomplished.

A. ventilation
B. spacing
C. work space
D. time delay

27. When a raceway is run from the interior to the exterior of a building, the raceway shall _____.

A. be rigid metal conduit (RMC)
B. be rigid nonmetallic conduit (RNC)
C. be sealed with an approved material
D. have an explosionproof seal

28. Where twenty (20) size 10 AWG copper current-carrying conductors with THHN insulation are installed in a 50 ft. run of trade size 1½ in. electrical metallic tubing (EMT), what is the allowable ampacity of each conductor?

A. 15 amperes
B. 20 amperes
C. 25 amperes
D. 30 amperes

29. Where flexible cord has one conductor identified by a ridge on the exterior of the cord, this conductor is identified as a/an _____ conductor.

A. ungrounded
B. grounded
C. phase
D. equipment grounding

30. Receptacles supplying power to freestanding-type office furnishings shall be located NOT more than _____ from the office furnishing that is connected to it.

A. 6 feet
B. 1 foot
C. 3 feet
D. 4 feet

31. Where multiple duplex receptacles are connected on a small-appliance branch circuit of a dwelling and protected by a 20-ampere rated circuit breaker, the receptacles are required to have an ampere rating of _____.

   I. 20 amperes
   II. 15 amperes

A. I only
B. II only
C. either I or II
D. neither I nor II

32. The full-load ampere rating of a motor relates to which of the following?

A. The locked-rotor current of the motor.
B. The starting current of the motor.
C. The torque current of the motor.
D. The running current of the motor at usual speed.

33. Unless listed and identified otherwise, terminations and conductors of circuits rated 100 amperes or larger, shall be rated for _____.

A. 60°C
B. 75°C
C. 90°C
D. 100°C

34. A feeder supplying two (2) continuous-duty, 208-volt, three-phase motors, one 10 hp and one 7½ hp shall have an ampacity of at LEAST _____.

A. 55.0 amperes
B. 68.75 amperes
C. 62.7 amperes
D. 38.5 amperes

35. GFCI protection for personnel is required where a 125-volt, single-phase, receptacle outlet is located on a wet bar countertop if within _____ of the outside edge of the sink.

A. 6 feet
B. 10 feet
C. 8 feet
D. 12 feet

Copyright © 2017

36. Which of the following conductor insulation types, if any, is/are acceptable for wiring in a fluorescent luminaire (lighting fixture) when the branch circuit conductors pass within three (3) inches of the ballast?

   I. THW
   II. THWN

A. I only
B. II only
C. both I and II
D. neither I nor II

37. In general, which of the following receptacles in a commercial kitchen are required by the NEC® to be GFCI protected?

A. All 125-volt 15- or 20-ampere rated receptacles.
B. All 125-volt 15- or 20-ampere rated receptacles in wet locations only.
C. All receptacles.
D. All 125-volt receptacles serving countertops and work surfaces only.

38. Cabinets containing overcurrent protection devices shall NOT be located _____.

A. over uneven surfaces
B. over a stairway landing
C. over steps of a stairway
D. under a mezzanine

39. The lightning protection system ground terminals shall be bonded to the building or structure grounding electrode system. The bonding shall be _____ and to all raceways, boxes, and enclosures between the cabinets or equipment and the grounding electrode.

A. insulated at both ends
B. insulated from one end
C. bonded at both ends
D. bonded at only one end

Copyright © 2017

40. Where concrete encased, raceways approved for burial only shall require a concrete envelope NOT less than _____ thick.

A. 2 inches
B. 4 inches
C. 6 inches
D. 8 inches

41. Where practicable, a separation of at LEAST _____ shall be maintained between communications wires and cables on buildings and lightning conductors.

A. 18 inches
B. 24 inches
C. 4 feet
D. 6 feet

42. Where appliances are likely to be used simultaneously, each _____ or fraction thereof of fixed multioutlet assemblies used in other than dwelling units shall be considered as an outlet of not less than 180 volt-amperes.

A. 24 inches
B. 36 inches
C. 5 feet
D. 12 inches

43. If the ampacity of the circuit conductors do not correspond with a standard size overcurrent protection device, and the load does NOT exceed_____, the next larger size overcurrent protection device is permitted to be used, if the conductors are not part of a branch circuit supplying more than one receptacle.

A. 60 amperes
B. 100 amperes
C. 200 amperes
D. 800 amperes

44. What is the MAXIMUM length permitted for use of flexible metallic tubing (FMT)?

A. 5 feet
B. 6 feet
C. 8 feet
D. 10 feet

45. As a general rule, where a cable is installed parallel to framing members, the cable shall be installed so that the nearest edge of the cable is NOT less than _____ from the nearest edge of the framing member.

A. ¾ in.
B. 1 in.
C. 1¼ in.
D. 1½ in.

46. What is the MINIMUM size 75 deg. C copper service-entrance conductors required for a 200 ampere rated commercial service?

A. 4/0 THW
B. 2/0 THW
C. 3/0 THHN
D. 3/0 THW

47. As per the NEC®, where multiple Type NM cables are bundled together for more than _____ the allowable ampacity of each conductor within the cable shall be reduced.

A. 30 inches
B. 24 inches
C. 36 inches
D. 48 inches

48. Additional services shall be permitted for a single building or other structure sufficiently large to make two (2) or more services necessary, if permitted by _____.

A. the registered design professional
B. qualified personnel
C. the engineer of record
D. special permission

49. Luminaires mounted in the walls of permanently installed swimming pools shall be installed with the top of the luminaire lens NOT less than _____ below the normal water level of the pool, unless the luminaire is listed and identified for use at lesser depths.

A. 18 inches
B. 6 inches
C. 24 inches
D. 12 inches

Copyright © 2017

50. Conductors tapped from a feeder and supplying a transformer need not have overcurrent protection if the length of the tap conductors are not over 25 ft. and have an ampacity of at LEAST_____ of the rating of the overcurrent device protecting the feeder conductors.

A. one-third
B. one-half
C. 80 percent
D. 75 percent

51. Automotive vacuum machines provided for public use at a commercial car wash, shall be protected by a _____.

A. GFCI only
B. GFCI and LCDI
C. GFCI and AFCI
D. GFCI, LCDI and AFCI

52. A hermetic motor-compressor that is protected against overloads by an inverse-time circuit breaker, shall be rated at NOT more than _____ of the motor-compressor full-load current.

A. 80%
B. 110%
C. 115%
D. 125%

53. Which one of the following listed wiring methods is NOT permitted to be installed in ducts specifically fabricated to transport environmental air?

A. flexible metallic tubing (FMT)
B. Type MI cable
C. electrical metallic tubing (EMT)
D. liquid-tight flexible metal conduit (LTFMC)

54. In regard to emergency and legally required standby systems, transfer switches shall be _____ and approved by the authority having jurisdiction.

A. manual
B. automatic
C. non-automatic
D. red in color

55. In industrial establishments where conditions of maintenance and supervision ensure that only qualified persons service the installation, flexible cords and cables are permitted to be installed in aboveground raceways having a length of NOT more than _____, to protect the cord or cable from physical damage.

A. 25 feet
B. 50 feet
C. 75 feet
D. 100 feet

56. In general, the power-supply cord to a mobile home shall be a feeder assembly consisting of not more than one listed _____ mobile home power-supply cord with a 3-pole, 4-wire, grounding type, 125/250-volt attachment plug cap.

A. 50 ampere
B. 60 ampere
C. 75 ampere
D. 100 ampere

57. Plate grounding electrodes shall be placed NOT less than _____ below the surface of the earth.

A. 30 inches
B. 24 inches
B. 18 inches
D. 12 inches

58. Where a 3 feet long electrical metallic conduit (EMT) will contain one (2) ungrounded conductors, one (1) grounded conductor and one (1) equipment grounding conductor, the conduit is permitted to be filled to a MAXIMUM of _____ of its cross-sectional area.

A. 53 percent
B. 31 percent
C. 40 percent
D. 60 percent

59. Where abandoned communications cables are identified for future use with a tag, the tag shall be _____.

A. red in color
B. orange in color
C. located outside of the junction box
D. of sufficient durability to withstand the environment involved

60. Determine the voltage drop on the size 14 AWG copper conductors of a 120-volt, single-phase branch circuit supplying a 10 ampere load located 60 feet from the source panelboard. (K = 12.9)

A. 3.76 volts
B. 7.52 volts
C. 3.26 volts
D. 7.36 volts

61. Where raceways contain insulated conductors of less than 1000 volts and of size _____ or larger enter a box or cabinet, the conductors must be provided with an insulating bushing, unless threaded hubs or bosses are used.

A. 10 AWG
B. 8 AWG
C. 6 AWG
D. 4 AWG

62. Which of the following is NOT required to be marked on the nameplate of a motor?

A. manufacturer's name
B. full-load current
C. overcurrent protection
D. rated temperature rise

63. Receptacles shall NOT be located less than _____ from the inside walls of a storable pool, storable spa, or storable hot tub.

A. 5 feet
B. 6 feet
C. 8 feet
D. 10 feet

64. Where exceptions are not applicable, when a metal pole supports a luminaire, the pole shall be provided with an accessible handhole NOT of less than _____ near the base of the pole to provide access to the supply terminations.

A. 2 in. x 6 in.
B. 3 in. x 4 in.
C. 2 in. x 4 in.
D. 4 in. x 6 in.

65. Messenger wire used to support 40 foot spans of overhead festoon lighting conductors of not more than 600 volts, shall be supported by _____.

A. porcelain knobs
B. strain insulators
C. racks
D. brackets

66. Where six (6) current-carrying conductors are contained in a common conduit or cable, the allowable ampacity of each of the current-carrying conductors shall be adjusted by a factor of _____.

A. 80 percent
B. 75 percent
C. 60 percent
D. 90 percent

67. What is demand load, in kW, on the ungrounded service conductors for one (1) single-phase, 240-volt, 9kW household electric range?

A. 9 kW
B. 7.2 kW
C. 8.8 kW
D. 8 kW

68. No underwater luminaires of swimming pools shall be installed for operation on supply circuits OVER _____ between conductors.

A. 15 volts
B. 120 volts
C. 125 volts
D. 150 volts

69. For continuous duty motors in a general application, the motor nameplate current rating is used to size the _____.

A. branch circuit conductors
B. overcurrent protection
C. overload protection
D. disconnecting means

70. When calculating the maximum number of conductors permitted in a conduit or tubing where all of the conductors are of the same size, an additional conductor of the same size is permitted in the conduit or tubing, when the calculation results in a decimal of at LEAST _____ or larger.

A. 0.75
B. 0.80
C. 0.50
D. 0.90

71. Conductors with type _____ insulation are NOT permitted to be installed in above grade raceways located outdoors where exposed to the weather.

A. THW
B. THWN
C. THHN
D. THWN-2

72. Where size 500 kcmil copper, 75°C rated conductors are used as ungrounded (phase) service-entrance conductors for a non-dwelling occupancy, what is the MAXIMUM standard size overcurrent protection permitted?

A. 380 amperes
B. 350 amperes
C. 375 amperes
D. 400 amperes

73. What is the MAXIMUM number of size 4 AWG THHN copper conductors permitted to be installed in a trade size 1¼ in. electrical metallic tubing (EMT) having a length of 18 inches?

A. 10
B. 11
C. 12
D. 13

Copyright © 2017

74. A type of an approved grounding electrode is a ground ring consisting of bare copper wire not smaller than 2 AWG, in direct contact with the earth for at LEAST _____ encircling the building or structure.

A. 10 feet
B. 20 feet
C. 30 feet
D. 50 feet

75. Given: A retail jewelry store has two (2) large show windows having a length of 15 feet each. One show window is on each side of the front entry door. How many single-phase, 125-volt, 15- or 20 ampere receptacle outlets must be provided for the show window lighting?

A. One per show window.
B. Two per show window.
C. Three per show window.
D. Four per show window.

76. A motor controller enclosure, rated not over 600 volts, that is subject to harsh environmental conditions such as rain, sleet, and snow is required to be a MINIMUM _____.

A. Type 3X
B. Type 6P
C. Type 12K
D. Type 3

77. Up to _____ sets of 3-wire feeders shall be permitted to utilize a common neutral.

A. two
B. three
C. four
D. five

78. Where direct-buried conductors emerge from below grade and extend up a pole, the conductors must be protected by enclosures or raceways up to a height of 8 feet above finished grade and in no case shall the protection be required to exceed _____ below finished grade.

A. 18 inches
B. 12 inches
C. 24 inches
D. 36 inches

Copyright © 2017

79. Given: A 120/240-volt, single-phase, one-family dwelling electrical service has a metal chain-link fence opposite exposed live parts of the service equipment. The required depth of the clear working space in front of the service equipment must be at LEAST _____.

A. 2½ feet
B. 4 feet
C. 3½ feet
D. 3 feet

80. Where a bedroom in a dwelling has a wall space of _____ or more in width (including space measured around corners) and unbroken along the floor line by doorways or similar openings, shall have a general-use receptacle outlet installed.

A. 6 feet
B. 12 feet
C. 2 feet
D. 4 feet

END OF JOURNEYMAN ELECTRICIANS FINAL EXAM

TEXAS ELECTRICIANS PRACTICE EXAMS
MASTER FINAL EXAM

This is an "open book" practice exam. A calculator and a 2017 edition of the NATIONAL ELECTRICAL CODE® is the only reference that should be used. This exam is typical of questions that may be encountered on the Texas Master Electrician licensing exams. Select the best answer from the choices given and review your answers with the answer key included in this book. Passing score on this practice exam is 75%. The exam consists of 100 questions valued at 1.00 point each, so you must answer at least 75 questions correct for a passing score. If you do not score at least 75% try again and keep studying.

ALLOTTED TIME: 5 hours

1. After all demand factors have been taken into consideration for an office building, the demand load is determined to be 90,000 VA. Where the building has a 120/240-volt, single-phase electrical system, what MINIMUM size copper conductors with THHW insulation is required for the ungrounded service-lateral conductors?

A. 400 kcmil
B. 350 kcmil
C. 300 kcmil
D. 500 kcmil

2. A commercial building is to be supplied with a transformer having a 480Y/277-volt, 3-phase primary and a 208Y/120-volt, 3-phase secondary. The secondary will have a balanced computed demand load of 416 amperes per phase. The transformer is required to have a MINIMUM kVA rating of _____.

A. 100 kVA
B. 150 kVA
C. 86 kVA
D. 200 kVA

3. An unbroken length of rigid metal conduit (RMC) or intermediate metal conduit (IMC) is permitted to support a luminaire of a billboard sign in lieu of a box where the:

A. luminaire is at least 8 feet above grade or standing area when accessible to unqualified persons.
B. length of conduit does not exceed 6 feet from the last point of conduit support.
C. conduit is of trade size 1 in. or larger.
D. total support weight on a single conduit does not exceed 30 pounds.

Copyright © 2017

4. The branch circuit conductors supplying one or more units of information technology equipment shall have an ampacity of NOT less than _____ of the total connected load.

A. 80 percent
B. 100 percent
C. 115 percent
D. 125 percent

5. In Class II, Division I hazardous locations, an approved method of connection of conduit to boxes is _____ .

A. compression fittings
B. threaded bosses
C. welding
D. all of these

6. Where a motor of more than 1 horsepower has a temperature rise of 50 deg. C indicated on the nameplate, for the purpose of selecting the overload device, this device shall be selected to trip at NO more than _____ of the motor's full-load ampere rating. (No exceptions or modifications permitted.)

A. 100 percent
B. 115 percent
C. 125 percent
D. 130 percent

7. For other than service conductors, to provide a reliable bonding connection, for circuits over _____ to ground, the electrical continuity of rigid metal conduit (RMC) or intermediate metal conduit (IMC) that enclose conductors shall be ensured with two locknuts, one inside and one outside of the enclosures.

A. 480 volts
B. 300 volts
C. 250 volts
D. 125 volts

8. Listed liquidtight flexible metal conduit (LFMC) is approved for use as an equipment grounding conductor if it does NOT exceed _____ in length.

A. 10 feet
B. 12 feet
C. 6 feet
D. 8 feet

9. Conductors supplying more than one (1) motor shall have an ampacity of NOT less than _____ of the full-load current rating of the highest rated motor in the group and 100% of the full-load current ratings of all the other motors in the group.

A. 125 percent
B. 110 percent
C. 150 percent
D. 175 percent

10. Where installed outdoors at carnivals, fairs or similar events, portable distribution and termination boxes shall be of weatherproof construction and mounted so the bottom of the enclosure is NOT less than _____ above the ground.

A. 6 inches
B. 8 inches
C. 10 inches
D. 12 inches

11. When intermediate metal conduit (IMC) is threaded in the field, a standard cutting die with a _____ taper per ft. shall be used.

A. 3/8 in.
B. 1/2 in.
C. 3/4 in.
D. 1 in.

12. Apply no exceptions and determine the MAXIMUM standard size nontime-delay fuse permitted for branch-circuit, short-circuit, and ground-fault protection for an ac motor where given the following related information:

* 2 hp – 120-volts, single-phase
* continuous-duty
* nameplate current rating - 22 amperes
* no code letter

A. 70 amperes
B. 80 amperes
C. 85 amperes
D. 90 amperes

13. The accessible portion of abandoned supply circuits and interconnecting cables located in an information technology equipment room shall be removed, unless _____.

Copyright © 2017

A. identified with a red colored tag
B. the conductors are size 10 AWG or larger
C. contained in a raceway
D. identified with a permanent tag

14. Under which if any, of the following conditions is the neutral conductor to be counted as a current-carrying conductor?

   I. When it is only carrying the unbalanced current of a single-phase system.
   II. When it is the neutral of a 3-phase wye-connected system that consists of nonlinear loads.

A. I only
B. II only
C. neither I nor II
D. both I and II

15. Indoor installed ceiling-suspended luminaires or paddle fans located _____ or more above the maximum water level of a spa or hot tub shall NOT require GFCI protection.

A. 10 feet
B. 7½ feet
C. 8 feet
D. 12 feet

16. A junction box to be installed will contain the following:

   * three - size 6 AWG ungrounded conductors
   * three - size 6 AWG grounded conductors
   * one - size 8 AWG equipment grounding conductor
   * three - size 12 AWG ungrounded conductors
   * three - size 12 AWG grounded conductors
   * one - size 12 equipment grounding conductor
   * four - internal clamps

The junction box is required to have a volume of at LEAST _____ .

A. 51.50 cubic inches   C. 46.50 cubic inches
B. 53.75 cubic inches   D. 56.50 cubic inches

17. Where conductors of size 4 AWG or larger are installed in conduits entering a junction box and straight pulls of the conductors are to be made, the length of the box shall NOT be less than _____ times the trade size of the largest raceway.

A. six
B. eight
C. ten
D. twelve

18. In motion picture studios, television studios and similar locations, each receptacle of dc plugging boxes shall be rated NOT less than how many amperes?

A. 15 amperes
B. 20 amperes
C. 25 amperes
D. 30 amperes

19. Electrical services and feeders for recreational vehicle parks shall be calculated on the basis of NOT less than _____ per RV site equipped with both 20-ampere and 30-ampere supply facilities.

A. 2400 volt-amperes
B. 9600 volt-amperes
C. 4800 volt-amperes
D. 3600 volt-amperes

20. Each operating room of a health care facility shall be provided with a MINIMUM of _____ hospital grade receptacles.

A. 36
B. 24
C. 18
D. 12

21. A disconnecting means that serves a hermetic refrigerant motor-compressor shall have an ampere rating of at LEAST _____ of the nameplate rated-load current or branch-circuit selection, whichever is greater.

A. 100 percent
B. 115 percent
C. 125 percent
D. 150 percent

Copyright © 2017

22. Where an electrical equipment room houses large equipment that contains overcurrent protective devices or switching devices, and the equipment is 1000 volts or less, rated 1,200 amperes or more and over 6 feet wide, for the purposes of entering and exiting the working space, two (2) entrances are required, one at each end. The doors are required to be not less than 6½ ft. high and NOT less than _____ wide.

A. 2 feet
B. 2½ feet
C. 3 feet
D. 3½ feet

23. Where a conductor is marked *RHW-2* on the insulation what does the *-2* represent?

A. The cable has 2 conductors.
B. The conductor is double insulated.
C. The conductor has a nylon outer jacket.
D. The conductor has a maximum operating temperature of 90 deg. C.

24. Type UF cable is NOT permitted for use _____.

A. underground
B. as a substitute for Type NM cable
C. as service-entrance cable
D. in cable trays

25. In a hospital, low-voltage equipment that is frequently in contact with the bodies of persons, must operate on a voltage of _____ or less or be moisture resistant, double insulated or approved as intrinsically safe.

A. 10 volts
B. 24 volts
C. 50 volts
D. 120 volts

26. A grounding electrode conductor or bonding jumper that is the sole connection to a rod, pipe, or plate electrode, and does not extend to other types of electrodes, shall NOT be required to be larger than size _____ copper conductor.

A. 1/0 AWG
B. 6 AWG
C. 4 AWG
D. 8 AWG

Copyright © 2017

27. A hazardous location where flammable gasses, flammable vapors, or combustible liquid-produced vapors may be present in the air in quantities sufficient to produce explosive or ignitible mixtures, is a _____ location.

A. Class I
B. Class II
C. Class III
D. Class IV

28. Where located in Class I, Division 1 locations, transformers containing oil or a liquid that will burn shall be _____.

A. enclosed in a fence
B. installed in vaults only
C. identified for Class I locations
D. installed in a fire-resistant room

29. In regard to commercial garages, lamps and lampholders for fixed lighting that is located over lanes through which vehicles are commonly driven shall be located NOT less than _____ above floor level, unless the luminaires are of the totally enclosed type.

A. 8 feet
B. 10 feet
C. 12 feet
D. 14½ feet

30. For nonshielded conductors of over 1000 volts, the conductors shall NOT be bent to a radius of less than _____ times the overall conductor material.

A. six
B. eight
C. ten
D. twelve

31. An adjustable overload protection device protecting a single phase, 240-volt, continuous-duty, 5 hp, ac motor with a FLA rating of 26 amperes and a temperature rise of 50 deg. C marked on the nameplate, shall be selected to trip at NOT more than _____ . (Consider the value you select will enable the motor to start without tripping and modification of this value is not necessary)

A. 29.9 amperes
B. 32.2 amperes
C. 33.8 amperes
D. 36.4 amperes

32. In Class II, Division 1 locations, where pendant mounted luminaires are suspended by rigid metal conduit (RMC) and a means for flexibility is not provided, the RMC stems shall have a length of NOT more than _____.

A. 12 inches
B. 18 inches
C. 24 inches
D. 30 inches

33. A commercial kitchen is to have the following cooking related equipment installed:

* one - 14 kW range
* one - 5.0 kW water heater
* one - 0.75 kW mixer
* one - 2.5 kW dishwasher
* one - 2.0 kW booster heater
* one - 2.0 kW broiler

Determine the demand load, in kW, after applying the demand factors for the kitchen equipment.

A. 19.00 kW
B. 26.25 kW
C. 18.38 kW
D. 17.06 kW

34. Portable lighting equipment used in Class I locations of a commercial repair garage shall be _____.

A. equipped with a switch
B. of conductive material
C. equipped with a means for plug-in of attachment plugs
D. of an unswitched type

35. Where a motor controller enclosure is located outdoors and is subject to be exposed to sleet, it shall have a MINIMUM rating of _____, where the controller mechanism is required to be operable when ice covered.

A. Type 3
B. Type 3S
C. Type 3R
D. Type 3SX

Copyright © 2017

36. When buried raceways pass under a commercial driveway or parking lot the MINIMUM cover requirements _____.

A. decrease if installed in rigid metal conduit (RMC)
B. do not change in regard to wiring methods used
C. shall be increased for direct-buried cables
D. shall be increased, decreased or remain the same, depending on the wiring method used

37. Given: A trade size 1 in. Schedule 40 PVC conduit is run horizontally out of the side of a panelboard for 50 feet, then turns at a 90° angle vertically for 40 feet where it enters the building through a LB conduit body. How many expansion fittings are required for this installation?

A. one
B. two
C. three
D. four

38. For other than Design B energy-efficient motors, where the setting specified in Table 430.52 of the NEC® is not sufficient for the starting current of the motor, the setting of an instantaneous trip circuit breaker shall be permitted to be increased, but in NO case exceed _____ of the full-load current of the motor.

A. 1300 percent
B. 1700 percent
C. 1100 percent
D. 800 percent

39. Where given the following related information, determine the MAXIMUM standard size overcurrent protection required for the primary and secondary side of a transformer, when primary and secondary overcurrent protection is to be provided.

   * 150 kVA rating
   * Primary – 480-volts, 3-phase, 3-wire
   * Secondary - 208Y/120-volts, 3-phase, 4-wire

A. Primary - 500 amperes, Secondary - 500 amperes
B. Primary - 450 amperes, Secondary - 600 amperes
C. Primary - 500 amperes, Secondary - 450 amperes
D. Primary - 450 amperes, Secondary - 500 amperes

Copyright © 2017

40. For capacitors of over 1000 volts, a means shall be provided to reduce the residual voltage of a capacitor to _____ after the capacitor is disconnected from the source of supply.

A. 50 volts or less within 1 minute
B. 24 volts or less within 1 minute
C. 50 volts or less within 10 minutes
D. 50 volts or less within 5 minutes

41. Apply no exceptions and determine the MAXIMUM standard size time-delay fuses permitted to be used for branch-circuit, short-circuit, and ground-fault protection for a 15 hp, 480-volt, three-phase, continuous-duty, wound rotor motor.

A. 30 amperes
B. 35 amperes
C. 40 amperes
D. 50 amperes

42. Generally, when conductors of different insulation ratings are installed in a common raceway and the voltage is 1000 volts or less, the NEC® requires _____.

A. all conductors shall have an insulation rating equal to at least the maximum circuit voltage applied to any conductor in the raceway
B. the conduit allowable fill to be limited to 31 percent
C. all conductors within the raceway shall have a temperature rating of 75°C
D. the insulation of the lower rated conductors to be identified with blue or yellow colors

43. Where used outdoors, aluminum grounding conductors shall NOT be terminated within _____ of the earth.

A. 18 inches
B. 24 inches
C. 3 feet
D. 6 feet

44. Given: An equipment disconnecting means is mounted at a height of 6 feet on a remote wall in an aircraft storage and maintenance hangar. The disconnect switch is 10 feet away from any aircraft fuel tanks. The disconnect switch is located in a/an _____ area.

A. Class II, Division 1
B. Class I, Division 2
C. Class I, Division 1
D. unclassified

45. Enclosures containing circuit breakers, switches and motor controllers located in Class II, Division 2 locations, shall be _____ or otherwise identified for the location.

A. gastight
B. vapor-proof
C. dusttight
D. stainless steel

46. Where installed for a commercial occupancy, determine the MINIMUM size THWN copper conductors required from the terminals of a 3-phase, 480Y/277-volt, 4-wire, 200 kW generator to the first distribution device(s) containing overcurrent protection. Assume the design and operation of the generator does NOT prevent overloading.

A. 250 kcmil
B. 300 kcmil
C. 400 kcmil
D. 500 kcmil

47. Where exceptions are not a consideration, each branch-circuit disconnect rated at LEAST _____ or more and installed on solidly grounded wye electrical systems of more than 150 volts to ground, but not exceeding 600 volts phase-to-phase, shall be provided with ground-fault protection of equipment.

A. 1500 amperes
B. 1000 amperes
C. 2000 amperes
D. 500 amperes

48. A dwelling unit to be built will have 1,400 sq. ft. of livable space on the main floor, a 1,400 sq. ft. basement (unfinished but adaptable for future use), a 200 sq. ft. open porch and a 600 sq. ft. garage. Determine the MINIMUM number of 15- ampere, 120-volt general lighting branch-circuits required for the dwelling.

A. four
B. five
C. six
D. seven

49. The optional method of feeder and service load calculations for dwelling units is reserved for feeder and service conductors with an ampacity of _____ or greater.

A. 400 amperes
B. 200 amperes
C. 150 amperes
D. 100 amperes

50. In an industrial establishment, what is the MAXIMUM length of 200 ampere rated busway that may be tapped to a 600 ampere rated busway, without additional overcurrent protection?

A. 10 feet
B. 25 feet
C. 50 feet
D. 75 feet

51. Thermal insulation is not permitted to be installed above a recessed luminaire or WITHIN _____ of the recessed luminaire's enclosure, wiring compartment, ballast, transformer, LED driver or power supply, unless the luminaire is identified as Type IC for insulation contact.

A. 3 inches
B. 4 inches
C. 6 inches
D. 8 inches

52. What is the MINIMUM height allowed for a fence enclosing an outdoor installation of 2,400 volt electrical equipment?

A. 6 feet
B. 7 feet
C. 8 feet
D. 9 feet

53. A listed _____ shall be installed in or on all emergency systems switchboards and panelboards.

A. surge-protective device (SPD)
B. ground-fault circuit interrupter (GFCI)
C. leakage-current detector-interrupter (LCDI)
D. arc-fault circuit interrupter (AFCI)

54. Storage batteries used as a source of power for emergency systems shall be of a suitable rating and capacity to supply and maintain the total load for at LEAST _____.

A. 1/2 hour
B. 1 hour
C. 1½ hours
D. 2 hours

55. Circuit breakers rated at _____ or less and 1000 volts or less shall have the ampere rating molded, stamped, etched or similarly marked into their handles or escutcheon areas.

A. 600 amperes
B. 200 amperes
C. 400 amperes
D. 100 amperes

56. The NEC® recommended MAXIMUM total voltage drop on both feeders and branch circuit conductors is _____.

A. 2 percent
B. 3 percent
C. 4 percent
D. 5 percent

57. A straight pull of size 250 kcmil and 350 kcmil conductors is to be made in a junction box that will have one (1) 3 in. conduit and two (2) 2½ in. conduits entering on the same side and exiting on the opposite wall. No splices or terminations will be made in the box. Which of the following listed junction boxes is the MINIMUM required for this installation?

A. 18 in. x 12 in.
B. 20 in. x 18 in.
C. 20 in. x 18 in.
D. 24 in. x 24 in.

58. Where conduits enter a floor-standing switchboard or panelboard at the bottom, the conduits, including their end fittings, shall NOT rise more than _____ above the bottom of the enclosure.

A. 6 inches
B. 3 inches
C. 2 inches
D. 4 inches

59. A bonding jumper connected between the communications grounding electrode and power grounding electrode system at the building or structure service where separate electrodes are used shall NOT be smaller than _____ copper.

A. 8 AWG
B. 6 AWG
C. 12 AWG
D. 10 AWG

60. Which of the following listed copper conductors, is the MINIMUM size 75°C rated conductors required to supply a continuous-duty, 25 hp, 208-volt, 3-phase motor, where the motor is on the end of a short conduit run that contains only three (3) conductors, at an ambient temperature of 115°F?

A. 1 AWG THWN
B. 2 AWG THWN
C. 1 AWG THHN
D. 1/0 AWG THWN

61. Single-conductor cable Type _____ shall be permitted in exposed outdoor locations in photovoltaic source circuits for photovoltaic module interconnections within the photovoltaic array.

A. UF
B. THHN
C. USE-2
D. THWN

62. All exposed non-current-carrying metal parts of an information technology system shall _____ or shall be double insulated.

A. be bonded to the equipment grounding conductor
B. not be bonded to the equipment grounding conductor
C. be bonded to the grounded conductor
D. be isolated

63. Where fixed wiring above bulk fuel storage tanks is installed in PVC conduit, the PVC shall be Schedule _____.

A. 20
B. 40
C. 80
D. 100

64. Disregarding exceptions, the MINIMUM size grounded or ungrounded conductors permitted to be connected in parallel (electrically joined at both ends) is _____.

A. 6 AWG
B. 1 AWG
C. 2 AWG
D. 1/0 AWG

65. Generally, 4 inch wide flat-top underfloor raceways shall have a covering of wood or concrete of NOT less than _____ above the raceway.

A. ½ in.
B. ¾ in.
C. 1 in.
D. 1¼ in.

66. Exposed trade size 3/4 in. Schedule 40 PVC conduit is required to be securely supported at intervals NOT to exceed _____.

A. 3 feet
B. 4 feet
C. 6 feet
D. 8 feet

Copyright © 2017

67. Given: A surge arrestor is required on each ungrounded service conductor of an industrial plant that experiences severe thunderstorms. If the electrical system is a 4-wire, wye-connected grounded system, how many surge arrestors are required?

A. four
B. three
C. two
D. one

68. When used as service-entrance conductors, size 250 kcmil Type IGS cable has an allowable ampacity of _____.

A. 215 amperes
B. 225 amperes
C. 119 amperes
D. 205 amperes

69. When exceptions are not a consideration, the MAXIMUM height above the floor or working platform to the center of the operating handle of a service disconnecting switch when it is in the *ON* position must NOT exceed _____.

A. 6 feet
B. 6 ft. 6 in.
C. 6 ft. 7 in.
D. 7 feet

70. The upward discharging vent of an underground fuel tank of motor fuel dispensing facilities is classified as a Class I, Division 1 location WITHIN _____ of the open vent.

A. 3 feet
B. 5 feet
C. 6 feet
D. 8 feet

71. Flexible metallic tubing (FMT) shall NOT be used in lengths exceeding _____.

A. 5 feet
B. 6 feet
C. 8 feet
D. 10 feet

72. Unless approved for a higher voltage, surface nonmetallic raceways are NOT approved where the voltage is _____ or more between conductors.

A. 120 volts
B. 150 volts
C. 300 volts
D. 250 volts

73. What is the MINIMUM permitted sill height of a transformer vault doorway?

A. 2 inches
B. 8 inches
C. 6 inches
D. 4 inches

74. What is the MAXIMUM number of times a wire-type grounding electrode conductor is permitted to be spliced by the use of split-bolt connectors?

A. one
B. two
C. three
D. none

75. Determine the MAXIMUM setting permitted for the overload protection for a 7½ hp, 3-phase, 480-volt, induction-type ac motor with a full-load current of 15 amperes, an 86% power factor, and a service factor of 1.00 indicated on the nameplate. (Assume exceptions and modifications are not to be applied.)

A. 17.25 amperes
B. 12.65 amperes
C. 18.75 amperes
D. 13.75 amperes

76. Where a surface-mounted luminaire containing a ballast, transformer, LED driver, or power supply is installed on combustible low-density cellulose fiberboard, it shall be marked for this condition or shall be spaced NOT less than _____ from the surface of the fiberboard.

A. ¾ in.
B. 1 in.
C. 1¼ in.
D. 1½ in.

Copyright © 2017

77. What is the MINIMUM bend radius of trade size 4 in. rigid metal conduit (RMC) where the bend is not made with a one-shot or full-shoe conduit bender?

A. 16 inches
B. 18 inches
C. 24 inches
D. 30 inches

78. A transformer is to be supplied with four (4) parallel size 500 kcmil conductors per phase. The conductors will enter the enclosure on the opposite wall of the terminals. What is the MINIMUM wire-bending space required for the conductors?

A. 10 inches
B. 12 inches
C. 14 inches
D. 16 inches

79. For trade size 3/4 in. Type MI cable, the radius of the inner edge of the bend shall NOT be less than _____ times the external diameter of the cable.

A. three
B. four
C. five
D. seven

80. Manhole covers shall be OVER _____ or otherwise designed to require the use of tools to open.

A. 25 lbs.
B. 50 lbs.
C. 75 lbs.
D. 100 lbs.

81. Size 4/0 AWG, 75°C aluminum secondary conductors of a 3-phase, delta-wye transformer, shall be protected at NOT more than _____ .

A. 175 amperes
B. 200 amperes
C. the calculated load connected to the transformer
D. none of these, because secondary protection is not required for multiphase, delta-wye transformer secondary conductors

82. For the purpose of determining conductor fill in conduit, a flexible cord or cable of four (4) conductors shall be treated as _____ conductor(s).

A. one
B. two
C. three
D. four

83. Where the grounding electrode system of a building or structure consists of three (3) driven ground rods, the ground rods shall be spaced NOT less than _____ apart.

A. 4 feet
B. 5 feet
C. 6 feet
D. 8 feet

84. What is the MAXIMUM size overcurrent protection device required to protect size 14 AWG copper conductors used for a pump motor control-circuit that is protected by the motor branch circuit protection device and extends beyond the enclosure?

A. 15 amperes
B. 20 amperes
C. 45 amperes
D. 100 amperes

85. What is the MAXIMUM number of size 12 AWG THHN conductors permitted to be installed in a trade size 3/8 in. flexible metal conduit (FMC) where the fittings are outside the FMC?

A. five
B. two
C. three
D. four

Copyright © 2017

86. A 120/240-volt, single-phase feeder of a retail shopping mall is to supply a noncontinuous load of 20,000 VA and a continuous load 16,000 VA. Consider the overcurrent device protecting the feeder conductors is not listed for operation at 100 percent of its rating and determine the MINIMUM size 75°C copper conductors required for this installation.

A. 1/0 AWG
B. 2/0 AWG
C. 3/0 AWG
D. 1 AWG

87. Apply the optional method of calculations for dwelling units and determine the demand load, in kW, on the ungrounded (line) service-entrance conductors for the electric ranges, where a 12 unit multifamily dwelling has an 8 kW range in each apartment.

A. 39.36 kW
B. 30.72 kW
C. 27.00 kW
D. 96.00 kW

88. An indoor installed 100 kVA, dry-type transformer with a 4,160-volt primary, must have a clearance of at LEAST _____ from combustible material unless separated from the combustible material by a fire-resistant, heat-insulated barrier.

A. 6 inches
B. 8 inches
C. 10 inches
D. 12 inches

89. When exceptions are not a consideration, interior metal water pipe that is electrically continuous with a metal underground water pipe electrode and is located NOT more than _____ from the point of entrance to the building shall be permitted to be used as a conductor to interconnect electrodes that are part of the grounding electrode system.

A. 10 feet
B. 8 feet
C. 5 feet
D. 20 feet

90. Given: A six (6) foot high metal chain-link fence topped with razor-wire, used to deter access by persons who are not qualified, encloses an outdoor installation of electrical apparatus rated 12 kV. The razor-wire shall be at LEAST _____ in height in order to comply with the NEC® rules.

A. 24 inches
B. 18 inches
C. 12 inches
D. 6 inches

91. What is the MINIMUM wire bending space required at the top and bottom of a panelboard that has one (1) size 3/0 AWG conductor connected to each busbar in the panelboard?

A. 6½ inches
B. 8 inches
C. 7½ inches
D. 6 inches

92. Power distribution blocks shall be permitted to be placed in pull and junction boxes having a volume over at LEAST _____ for connections of conductors installed in boxes where the power distribution blocks do not have uninsulated live parts exposed within the box, whether or not the box cover is installed.

A. 30 cu. in.
B. 60 cu. in.
C. 75 cu. in.
D. 100 cu. in.

93. In a health care facilities patient bed location, each patient bed location in Category 1 and Category 2 spaces shall be supplied by at least two (2) branch circuits, and the branch circuits serving the patient bed locations _____.

A. should be AFCI protected
B. shall not be part of a multiwire branch circuit
C. must have isolated equipment grounded conductors
D. should supply only single receptacle outlets

94. A flexible metal conduit (FMC) having a length of 4 feet is to supply a panelboard from a transformer. The FMC will contain three (3) size 400 kcmil THWN copper conductors and one (1) size 350 kcmil THWN copper conductor. In compliance with the NEC®, what is the MINIMUM trade size FMC required?

A. 2½ in.
B. 3 in.
C. 3½ in.
D. 4 in.

95. An outside overhead span of 3-phase, 4-wire, 480Y/277-volt conductors are to be installed between two buildings of a college campus. The area the conductors cross will not be subject to truck traffic. The conductors must have a MINIMUM clearance of _____ from final grade.

A. 10 feet
B. 12 feet
C. 15 feet
D. 18 feet

96. Cables operating at over 1000 volts and those operating at 1000 volts or less, are permitted to be installed in a common cable tray without a fixed barrier, where the cables operating at over 1000 volts are _____.

A. Type MI
B. Type NM
C. Type CT
D. Type MC

97. A thermal barrier shall be required if the space between resistors and reactors and any combustible material is LESS than _____.

A. 6 inches
B. 8 inches
C. 12 inches
D. 18 inches

98. Where a restaurant located in a retail shopping mall has a main circuit breaker rated for 400 amperes, the required bonding jumper to the metal water piping system is to be at LEAST _____ copper.

A. 6 AWG
B. 2 AWG
C. 3 AWG
D. 4 AWG

99. In general, on the load side of the point of grounding of a separately derived system such as a transformer, a grounded conductor is NOT permitted to be connected to _____.

A. equipment grounding conductors
B. normally non-current-carrying metal parts of equipment
C. the system bonding jumper
D. any of these

100. Where one or more 125-volt, single-phase, 15- or 20-ampere receptacle outlets are provided for the show window lighting in a retail store, the outlet(s) shall be installed within at LEAST _____ of the top of the show window.

A. 12 inches
B. 18 inches
C. 24 inches
D. 30 inches

END OF MASTER ELECTRICIAN FINAL EXAM

Notes

Copyright © 2017

Notes

ANSWER KEYS
WITH NEC® REFERENCES

TEXAS ELECTRICIANS PRACTICE EXAMS
MAINTENANCE ELECTRICIAN
PRACTICE EXAM #1
ANSWER KEY

ANSWER	REFERENCE	NEC PG. #
1. B	90.1(A)	pg. 30
2. B	Article 100 - Definitions	pg. 35
3. A	Article 100 - Definitions	pg. 38
4. B	General Knowledge	
5. A	General Knowledge	
6. C	Trade Knowledge	
7. C	Article 100 - Definitions	pg. 39
8. A	Article 100 - Definitions	pg. 33
9. B	Table 430.250	pg. 322
10. C	Chapter 9, Table 1	pg. 679
11. B	Table 110.26(A)(1)	pg. 47
12. D	310.106(C)	pg. 170
13. D	Article 100 - Definitions	pg. 37
14. A	Table 240.6(A)	pg. 95
15. B	Table 314.16(A)	pg. 176
16. D	362.30(A)	pg. 213
17. D	210.21(B)(1)	pg. 62
18. C	430.6(A)(1) Table 430.248 430.22	pg. 297 pg. 321 pg. 302

FLC of 7½ hp motor = 40 amperes x 125% = 50 amperes

19. A	Table 310.15(B)(16)	pg. 150
20. B	240.51(B)	pg. 99

21. C   Single-phase current formula

$$I = \frac{Power}{Volts} \quad I = \frac{10 \text{ kW} \times 1{,}000}{240 \text{ volts}} = \frac{10{,}000}{240} = 41.6 \text{ amperes}$$

22. D   Chapter 9, Table 8   pg. 689
                         Voltage Drop Formula

$$VD = \frac{2 \times K \times I \times D}{CM}$$

$$VD = \frac{2 \times 12.9 \times 50 \times 150}{26{,}240} = \frac{193{,}500}{26{,}240} = 7.37 \text{ volts dropped}$$

23. A   Chapter 9, Table 8   pg. 689
                         Wire Size Formula

1st. find VD permitted -   240 volts x 3% = 7.2 volts

$$CM = \frac{2 \times K \times I \times D}{VD}$$

$$CM = \frac{2 \times 12.9 \times 40 \times 100}{7.2} = \frac{103{,}200}{7.2} = 14{,}333 \text{ CM}$$

NOTE* A size 8 AWG conductor with a CMA of 16,510 should be selected.

24. B   Single-phase current Formula

$$I = \frac{Power}{Volts} \quad I = \frac{150 \text{ watts} \times 15 \text{ (lights)}}{120 \text{ volts}} = \frac{2250}{120} = 18.75 \text{ amperes}$$

25. D   404.8(A)   pg. 255

##

Copyright © 2017

TEXAS ELECTRICIANS PRACTICE EXAMS
MAINTENANCE ELECTRICIAN
PRACTICE EXAM #2
ANSWER KEY

ANSWER	REFERENCE	NEC PG. #
1. D	210.19(A)(1)(a)	pg. 62

Single-phase power Formula

$$\frac{20 \text{ amperes}}{125\%} = 16 \text{ amperes}$$

$P = I \times E \quad P = 20 \text{ amperes} \times 120 \text{ volts} = \dfrac{2400 \text{ VA}}{125\%} = 1920 \text{ VA}$

2. C	110.26(A)(2)	pg. 47
3. A	90.1(B)	pg. 30
4. A	Trade knowledge	
5. C	430.7(A)(1),(2)&(5)	pg. 298
6. A	110.26(F)	pg. 49
7. D	110.15	pg. 43
8. B	220.14(I)	pg. 71
9. A	Table 310.15(B)(3)(a)	pg. 148
10. B	300.20(A)	pg. 141
11. A	358.30(A)	pg. 210
12. B	430.109(C)(2)	pg. 315
13. C	430.6(A)(2)	pg. 298
14. A	430.22	pg. 302
15. A	250.119	pg. 123
16. C	240.83(D)	pg. 100

Copyright © 2017

17. C 210.5(C)(1) pg. 57

18. B 200.11 pg. 57

19. C 3-Phase Current Formula

$$I = \frac{kW \times 1{,}000}{Volts \times 1.732}$$

$$I = \frac{9kW \times 1{,}000}{208 \times 1.732} = \frac{9{,}000 \text{ watts}}{360.25} = 24.9 \text{ amperes}$$

20. B Chapter 9, Table 8 pg. 689
       Distance Formula

1st. find allowable VD - 240 volts x 3% = 7.2 volts

$$D = \frac{CM \times VD}{2 \times K \times I} \quad D = \frac{16{,}510 \times 7.2}{2 \times 12.9 \times 42} = \frac{118{,}872}{1{,}083.6} = 109.7 \text{ ft.}$$

21. B 348.20(A)(2)c. pg. 199

22. B 300.6(D) pg. 138

23. A 210.19(A)(1)(a) pg. 62

24. C Table 210.21(B)(3) pg. 63

25. B 240.4(D)(5) pg. 94

###

Copyright © 2017

TEXAS ELECTRICIANS PRACTICE EXAMS
RESIDENTIAL WIREMAN
PRACTICE EXAM #3
ANSWER KEY

ANSWER	REFERENCE	NEC PG. #
1. D	210.52(4)	pg. 64
2. B	210.8(A)(2) 210.12(A)	pg. 59 pg. 60
3. C	680.71	pg. 555
4. C	410.16(C)(1)	pg. 268
5. A	210.50(C)	pg. 64
6. A	410.30(A)	pg. 269
7. C	422.11(E)(3) Table 240.6(A) Single-phase current formula	pg. 277 pg. 95

$$I = \frac{Watts}{Volts} \quad I = \frac{4500 \text{ watts}}{240 \text{ volts}} = 18.75 \text{ amperes} \times 150\% = 28.1 \text{ amperes}$$

NOTE* The next standard size circuit breaker with a rating of 30 amperes should be selected.

8. A	410.117(C)	pg. 272
9. D	250.52(A)(1)	pg. 112
10. D	General knowledge Current formula	

$$I = \frac{kVA \times 1,000}{Volts} \quad I = \frac{175 \text{ kVA} \times 1,000}{240 \text{ volts}} = \frac{175,000 \text{ VA}}{240} = 729.1 \text{ amperes}$$

11. B	340.10(4) 334.30	pg. 195 pg. 192
12. C	Table 220.12	pg. 71

70 ft. x 30 ft. = 2100 sq. ft. x 3 VA = 6300 VA (house load)
120 volts x 15 amperes   = 1800 VA (one circuit)

$\frac{6300 \text{ VA (load)}}{1800 \text{ VA (circuit)}}$ = 3.5 = 4 15 ampere general lighting circuits

Copyright © 2017

13. C	Table 210.21(B)(3)	pg. 63
14. B	210.52(A)(3)	pg. 64
15. D	210.11(C)(1)-(4)	pg. 60
16. A	Article 100 - Definitions	pg. 33
17. A	Table 240.6(A)	pg. 95
18. B	240.24(E)	pg. 99
19. B	Article 100 - Definitions	pg. 40
20. A	210.52(H)	pg. 66
21. D	210.52(C)(1)	pg. 65
22. B	Table 300.5, Column 4	pg. 137
23. C	334.15(C)	pg. 192
24. B	210.52(G)(1)	pg. 66
25. B	404.2(A)	pg. 254

##

TEXAS ELECTRICIANS PRACTICE EXAMS
RESIDENTIAL WIREMAN
PRACTICE EXAM #4
ANSWER KEY

ANSWER	REFERENCE	NEC PG. #
1. C	210.52(C)(5)	pg. 65
2. B	404.14(E)	pg. 257
3. C	210.19(A)(3)	pg. 62
4. A	110.6	pg. 44
5. C	422.16(B)(1)(2)	pg. 278
6. B	314.16(B)(1),(2),(4)&(5) Table 314.16(B)	pgs. 175 & 176 pg. 176

```
size 14 AWG    = 2.00 cu. in. x 4 = 8.00 cu. in.
size 12 AWG    = 2.25 cu. in. x 4 = 9.00 cu. in.
equip grnd.    = 2.25 cu. in. x 1 = 2.25 cu. in.
clamps         = 2.25 cu. in. x 1 = 2.25 cu. in.
receptacle.    = 2.25 cu. in. x 2 = 4.50 cu. in.
switch         = 2.00 cu. in. x 2 = 4.00 cu. in.
                         TOTAL = 30.00 cu. in.
```

COMMENT: Clamps, 1 or more, are counted as equal to the largest wire in the box. 314.16(B)(2) Equipment grounding conductors, 1 or more, are counted as equal to the largest equipment grounding conductor in the box. 314.16(B)(5) Devices are counted as equal to two conductors, based on the largest conductor connected to the device. 314.16(B)(4)

7. B	680.22(A)(2)	pg. 546
8. D	406.4(C)	pg. 258
9. B	210.23(A)(1)	pg. 63

20 amperes x 80% = 16 amperes

10. A	422.11(E)(3) Current Formula Table 240.6(A)	pg. 277 pg. 95

$$I = \frac{VA}{volts} \quad I = \frac{9600 \text{ VA}}{240 \text{ volts}} = 40 \text{ amperes} \times 150\% = 60 \text{ amperes}$$

Copyright © 2017

11. C	230.79(C)	pg. 90
12. A	Table 220.55 & Note 3	pg. 74

    Use column B - 5 appliances = 45% demand

    6.0 kW
    8.0 kW
    3.5 kW
    6.0 kW
    <u>3.5 kW</u>
    27 kW (total connected load)

    27 kW x 45% = 12.15 kW (demand load)

13. B	Article 100 - Definitions	pg. 34
14. A	300.4(A)(2)	pg. 135
15. B	Table 250.66	pg. 116
	250.66(B)	pg. 115
16. C	250.52(B)(1)	pg. 113
17. B	314.16(B)(3)	pg. 176
18. C	310.15(B)(3)(a)	pg. 147
19. A	310.15(B)(7)(1)	pg. 149
20. D	Table 220.54	pg. 73
21. A	340.80	pg. 196
22. A	314.20	pg. 177
23. B	310.15(B)(7)(1)	pg. 149
	Table 310.15(B)(16)	pg. 150

    150 amperes x .83 = 124.5 amperes
    Size 1 AWG conductors with an ampacity of 130 amperes should be selected from Table 310.15(B)(16).

24. B	Table 210.21(B)(2)	pg. 63
25. D	300.14	pg. 140

###

Copyright © 2017

TEXAS ELECTRICIANS PRACTICE EXAMS
RESIDENTIAL WIREMAN
PRACTICE EXAM #5
ANSWER KEY

ANSWER	REFERENCE	NEC. PG. #
1. A	422.16(B)(2)(3)	pg. 278
2. B	220.53	pg. 73
3. C	314.27(C)	pg. 179
4. B	250.68(A), Exception 1	pg. 115
5. C	240.24(D)&(E)	pg. 99
6. C	Table 314.16(A)	pg. 176
7. C	220.12 Table 220.12	pg. 70 pg. 71

2,600 sq. ft. x 3 VA = 7,800 VA (total lighting VA of house)
120 volts x 15 amperes = 1,800 VA (one circuit VA)

$\dfrac{7{,}800 \text{ VA (load)}}{1{,}800 \text{ VA (one circuit)}}$ = 4.3 = 5 – 15 ampere lighting circuits

8. B	408.41	pg. 264
9. C	210.52(A)(1)	pg. 64
10. C	220.53	pg. 73

6 x 5 kW = 30 kW x 75% (demand factor) = 22.5 kW demand

11. D	210.52(D)	pg. 65
12. C	300.4(D)	pg. 135
13. A	314.16(B)(5)	pg. 176
14. D	Table 310.104(A) 310.10(B)&(C)(2)	pg. 168 pg. 145
15. D	680.43(B)(1)(a)	pg. 552
16. C	220.54	pg. 73

Copyright © 2017

- 180 -

17. C   210.23(B)   pg. 63

   30 amperes x 80% = 24 amperes

18. A   240.4(D)(5)   pg. 94

19. D   Table 220.55 & Note 3   pg. 74

   Use column B - 2 appliances = 65% demand
   5 kW + 7 kW = 12 kW (total connected load)
   12 kW x 65% = 7.8 kW (demand load)

20. A   Table 250.122   pg. 125
21. A   210.52(A)(2)(1)   pg. 64
22. C   210.63   pg. 66
23. A   200.6(B)(4)   pg. 55
24. B   410.116(A)(1)   pg. 272
25. C   210.8(A)(1),(2)&(3)   pg. 59

##

Copyright © 2017

**TEXAS ELECTRICIANS PRACTICE EXAMS
RESIDENTIAL WIREMAN
PRACTICE EXAM #6
ANSWER KEY**

ANSWER	REFERENCE	NEC. PG. #
1. C	210.8(D) 210.12(A)	pg. 59 pg. 60
2. B	230.26	pg. 86
3. C	Table 110.26(A)(1)	pg. 47
4. B	225.18(2)	pg. 80
5. A	680.43(C)	pg. 552
6. D	680.22(A)(4)	pg. 546
7. D	314.27(A)(2)	pg. 179
8. A	250.8(A)	pg. 106
9. C	250.53(G)	pg. 113
10. A	230.51(A)	pg. 88
11. D	210.52(C)(1)	pg. 65
12. B	680.34	pg. 551
13. C	680.26(B) 680.26(B)(1)(a)	pg. 549 pg. 549
14. B	Table 300.5, Column 2	pg. 137
15. C	210.70(A)(2)(3)	pg. 67
16. B	Table 210.21(B)(3)	pg. 63
17. D	250.64(C)(1)	pg. 114

Copyright © 2017

18. B   Table 220.55, Column C   pg. 74
                                210.19(A)(3)   pg. 62

Single-phase current formula

$$I = \frac{8 \text{ kW} \times 1000}{240 \text{ volts}} = \frac{8,000}{240} = 33.3 \text{ amperes}$$

However, Section 210.19(A)(3) states …. For ranges having a rating of 8.75 kW or more the minimum branch circuit rating shall be 40 amperes.

19. A   250.68(C)(1)   pg. 116

20. B   210.52(C)(2)   pg. 65

21. C   240.24(F)   pg. 99

22. C   Table 314.16(B)   pg. 176

23. B   334.30   pg. 192

24. D   210.8(A)(7)   pg. 59

25. B   Table 314.16(B)   pg. 176
                               314.16(B)(4)   pg. 176

18 cu. in.(box) / 2.25 cu. in.(#12 wire) = 8 wires (allowable fill)
                                             <u>-2 wires (device)</u>
                                         6 wires may be added

* NOTE: A size 12/2 AWG with ground NM cable contains three (3) conductors.

$$\frac{6 \text{ wires (may be added)}}{3 \text{ (wires in NM cable)}} = 2 \text{ size 12/2 NM cables may be installed}$$

###

TEXAS ELECTRICIANS PRACTICE EXAMS
JOURNEYMAN ELECTRICIAN
PRACTICE EXAM #7
ANSWER KEY

ANSWER	REFERENCE	NEC PG. #
1. A	Table 430.52	pg. 308
	430.52(C)(1), Exception 1	pg. 307
2. A	404.14(B)(2)	pg. 257
3. D	Table 314.16(B)	pg. 176

#12 AWG conductors – 2.25 cu. in. x 5 = 11.25 cu. in.
#10 AWG conductors – 2.50 cu. in. x 6 = 15.00 cu. in.
Total = 26.25 cu. in.

4. A	Table 680.9(A)	pg. 545
5. C	410.12	pg. 268
6. D	Table 344.30(B)(2)	pg. 199
7. D	220.12	pg. 70
8. A	Article 100 - Definitions	pg. 38
9. B	300.34	pg. 143
10. C	300.6(A)	pg. 138
11. A	Table 352.30	pg. 203
12. B	Table 310.15(B)(16)	pg. 150
	Table 310.15(B)(2)(a)	pg. 147
	Table 310.15(B)(3)(a)	pg. 148

250 THWN copper ampacity before derating = 255 amperes
255 amps x .82 (temp. correction) x .8 (adj. factor) = 167.28 amperes

13. C	310.10(H)(1)	pg. 146
14. D	410.136(B)	pg. 274
15. A	368.30	pg. 216
16. D	502.10(A)(1)&(2)	pg. 364
17. B	368.17(A), Exception 1	pg. 216

Copyright © 2017

	240.4(C)	pg. 94
	Table 240.6(A)	pg. 95
18. A	430.6(A)(1)	pg. 297
19. D	250.64(E)(1)	pg. 115
20. A	300.5(D)(1)	pg. 136
21. C	605.9(B)	pg. 496
22. B	530.14	pg. 448
23. C	422.11(C)	pg. 276
24. B	430.32(A)(1)	pg. 304
25. D	Table 430.37	pg. 306

##

TEXAS ELECTRICIANS PRACTICE EXAMS
JOURNEYMAN ELECTRICIAN
PRACTICE EXAM #8
ANSWER KEY

ANSWER	REFERENCE	NEC PG. #
1. B	625.50	pg. 613
2. C	430.6(A)(2)	pg. 298
3. B	Table 511.3(C)	pg. 394
4. B	430.22	pg. 302
5. D	Table 430.52	pg. 308
6. D	300.5(B)	pg. 136
7. D	430.81(B)	pg. 312
8. C	Table 430.250 430.22	pg. 322 pg. 302

FLC of motor = 30.8 amperes x 125% = 38.5 amperes

9. C	410.10(F)	pg. 268
10. A	210.23(A)(2)	pg. 63
11. D	Chapter 9, Note 4 to Tables	pg. 679
12. A	210.11(C)(4), Exception	pg. 60
13. C	314.16(B)(1) Table 314.16(B)	pg. 175 pg. 176

Size 12 AWG - 2.25 cu. in. x 4 wires =   9 cu. in.
Size 10 AWG - 2.50 cu. in. x 4 wires = 10 cu. in.
                    TOTAL = 19 cu. in.

14. B	390.4(A)	pg. 227
15. A	Table 314.16(A)	pg. 176
16. A	310.15(B)(3)(a)(2)	pg. 147
17. C	240.83(B)	pg. 100

Copyright © 2017

18. C	Table 310.104(A)	pg. 167
19. C	324.1	pg. 184
20. B	225.18(1)	pg. 80
21. C	Table 310.104(A) 310.10(B)&(C)(2)	pg. 167 pg. 145
22. C	230.23(B)	pg. 85
23. C	110.26(C)(2)	pg. 48
24. D	110.26(A)(2)	pg. 47
25. A	680.23(A)(5)	pg. 547

###

TEXAS ELECTRICIANS PRACTICE EXAMS
JOURNEYMAN ELECTRICIAN
PRACTICE EXAM #9
ANSWER KEY

ANSWER	REFERENCE	NEC PG. #
1. C	Table 110.28	pg. 50
2. B	250.102(C)(1)	pg. 118
	Table 250.102(C)(1)	pg. 119
3. A	502.115(B)	pg. 366
4. C	310.10(H)(2)(1)&(3)	pg. 146
5. D	Table 310.15(B)(16)	pg. 150
	Table 310.15(B)(3)(a)	pg. 148

1/0 THW ampacity (before derating) = 150 amps x 80% (adj. factor) = 120 amps

6. D	3-phase power formula	

First find VA – 208 volts x 1.732 x 243 amperes = 87,542 VA
87,542 VA ÷ 1,000 = 87.5 kVA

7. D	430.6(A)(1)	pg. 297
	Table 430.248	pg. 321
	Table 430.52	pg. 308
	430.52(C)(1),Exception 1	pg. 307
	Table 240.6(A)	pg. 95

FLC of motor = 28 amperes [Table 430.248]
28 amperes x 300% = 84 amperes   [Table 430.52]

*NOTE - You are permitted to go up to the next standard size fuses
with a rating of 90 amperes. [430.52(C)(1), Exception 1]

8. C	240.4(B)(2)&(3)	pg. 94
	Table 240.6(A)	pg. 95
9. C	Chapter 9, Table 8	pg. 689
	Voltage Drop Formula	

$$VD = \frac{2 \times K \times I \times D}{CM} \quad VD = \frac{2 \times 12.9 \times 20 \times 150}{10,380} = 7.45 \text{ volts dropped}$$

Copyright © 2017

10. D	430.24(1)&(2)	pg. 303
11. B	Annex C, Table C.1	pg. 713
12. A	310.15(B)(5)(a)&(b)	pg. 148
13. A	225.4	pg. 78
14. C	314.28(A)(1)	pg. 180
15. C	Article 100 Definitions	pg. 35
16. D	392.20(B)(1)	pg. 230
17. D	680.23(B)(2)(a)&(b)	pg. 547
18. B	300.22(C)(1)	pg. 142
19. A	422.11(E)(1)-(3)	pg. 277
20. C	Table 110.26(A)(1)	pg. 47
21. D	680.56(B)	pg. 554
	Table 400.4	pg. 245
22. B	410.68	pg. 271
23. C	300.4(G)	pg. 136
24. C	500.5(D)	pg. 351
25. A	Table 310.15(B)(16)	pg. 150
	Table 310.15(B)(2)(a)	pg. 147

Size 2 AWG @ 75 deg. C ampacity (before derating) = 115 amperes
115 amperes x .88 (temp. derating factor) = 101 amperes

##

Copyright © 2017

TEXAS ELECTRICIANS PRACTICE EXAMS
JOURNEYMAN ELECTRICIAN
PRACTICE EXAM #10
ANSWER KEY

ANSWER	REFERENCE	NEC PG. #
1. B	424.36	pg. 283
2. D	Article 100 - Definitions	pg. 38
3. B	220.14(I)	pg. 71
4. B	210.52(C)(1)	pg. 65
	210.52(C)(4)	pg. 65
5. B	250.35(A)	pg. 111
	250.30(A)(1)	pg. 108
6. A	Figure 514.3	pg. 398
7. C	314.28(A)(1)	pg. 180

12 in. (box) ÷ 8 (raceway) = 1.5 or 1½ inches

8. A	Trade knowledge	
9. C	430.24(1)&(2)	pg. 303

10 amps x 100% = 10.0 amperes
20 amps x 100% = 20.0 amperes
30 amps x 125% = <u>37.5 amperes</u>
TOTAL = 67.5 amperes

10. C	220.14(F)	pg. 71
	600.5(B)	pg. 488
	210.19(A)(1)(a)	pg. 62

1,200 VA x 125% = 1,500 VA

11. D	Table 430.250	pg. 322
	430.22	pg. 309
	Table 310.15(B)(16)	pg. 150

FLC of motor – 80 amperes x 125% = 100 amperes
Size 3 AWG THW conductors with an ampacity of 100 amperes should be Selected from Table 310.15(B)(16).

Copyright © 2017

12. D	460.28(A)	pg. 340
13. C	440.14	pg. 326
14. C	250.118(5)(a)-(e)	pg. 122
15. B	440.22(A)	pg. 327

        18 amperes x 225% = 40.5 amperes

16. B	348.30(A)	pg. 200
17. A	700.12(B)(2)	pg. 585
18. C	332.30	pg. 190
19. B	680.22(B)(1)	pg. 546
20. A	430.32(A)(1)	pg. 304
	430.32(C)	pg. 305
21. C	300.9	pg. 139
	310.10(B)&(C)	pg. 145
22. C	230.95	pg. 91
23. A	Table 310.15(B)(16)	pg. 150
	Table 310.15(B)(2)(a)	pg. 147
	Table 310.15(B)(3)(a)	pg. 148

    500 kcmil THWN copper ampacity before derating = 380 amperes
    380 amps x .67 (temp. correction) x .7 (adj. factor) = 178.22 amperes

24. B	340.10(1)&(4)	pg. 195
	340.12(1)	pg. 196
25. D	406.3(D)	pg. 258

##

Copyright © 2017

TEXAS ELECTRICIANS PRACTICE EXAMS
JOURNEYMAN ELECTRICIAN
PRACTICE EXAM #11
ANSWER KEY

ANSWER	REFERENCE	NEC PG. #
1. C	250.106	pg. 120
2. A	230.9(A)	pg. 85
3. A	250.64(A)	pg. 114
4. A	Article 100 - Definitions	pg. 34
5. B	555.22 Table 511.3(C)	pg. 484 pg. 394
6. C	110.6	pg. 44
7. C	250.66(B)	pg. 115
8. C	422.11(E)(3)	pg. 277

20 amperes x 150% = 30 amperes

9. B	110.14(C) Table 310.15(B)(16) Table 310.15(B)(2)(a)	pg. 45 pg. 150 pg. 147

3 AWG THHN ampacity before derating = 115 amps (90 deg. C Column)
115 amperes x .96 (temperature correction) = 110.4 amperes.
3 AWG (60 deg. C Col.) = 85 amperes is to be used because the terminations are rated for 60ºC.

10. A	90.5(A)	pg. 31
11. B	Table 352.30	pg. 203
12. A	450.21(B)	pg. 335
13. B	392.10(B)(1)(a)	pg. 228
14. D	440.65	pg. 329
15. C	320.108	pg. 183
16. C	445.13	pg. 330

Copyright © 2017

17. D	300.13(B)	pg. 139
18. B	210.60(B)	pg. 66
19. A	240.8	pg. 95
20. D	200.4(A)	pg. 55
21. A	250.66(A)	pg. 115
22. A	Table 630.11(A)	pg. 519
	Table 310.15(B)(16)	pg. 150

.78 (duty cycle) x 50 amperes (primary current) = 39 amperes
Tbl. 310.15(B)(16) requires size 8 AWG 60°C rated conductors.

23. A	300.4(A)(2)	pg. 135
24. C	210.62	pg. 66
25. B	400.12(2)	pg. 250

##

TEXAS ELECTRICIANS PRACTICE EXAMS
JOURNEYMAN ELECTRICIAN
PRACTICE EXAM #12
ANSWER KEY

ANSWER	REFERENCE	NEC PG. #
1. A	Chapter 9, Table 5	pg. 685

    4/0 AWG THWN - .3237 sq. in. x 3 = .9711 sq. in.
    3/0 AWG THWN - .2679 sq. in. x 1 = .2679 sq. in.
    4 AWG THWN   - .0824 sq. in. x 1 = .0824 sq. in.
                     TOTAL   1.3214 sq. in.

2. C	334.116(B)	pg. 193
3. B	430.110(A)	pg. 315
4. C	215.2(A)(1)(a)	pg. 67

    240 amperes x 125 % = 300 amperes

5. D	220.12	pg. 70
	Table 220.12	pg. 71

    12,000 sq. ft. x 2 VA = 24,000 VA (building lighting VA)
    120 volts x 20 amperes   = 2,400 VA (one circuit VA)
    24,000 VA (blg.) ÷ 2,400 VA (one circuit) = 10 general lighting circuits

6. D	Chapter 9, Table 8	pg. 689
	Single-phase voltage drop formula	

$$VD = \frac{2KID}{CM} \quad\quad VD = \frac{2 \times 12.9 \times 80 \text{ amps} \times 200 \text{ ft.}}{52,620 \text{ CM}} = 7.84 \text{ volts}$$

7. B	501.15(A)(1)	pg. 357
8. D	300.3(C)(1)	pg. 134
9. A	400.17	pg. 250
10. C	250.102(D)	pg. 119
11. A	680.74(A)(1)&(2)	pg. 555

Copyright © 2017

12. B General Knowledge
3-Phase Current Formula

$$I = \frac{\text{Power}}{\text{Volts} \times 1.732}$$

$$I = \frac{90 \text{ kVA} \times 1000}{208 \text{ volts} \times 1.732} = \frac{90{,}000 \text{ VA}}{360.25} = 250 \text{ amperes}$$

13. A   430.6(A)(1)   pg. 297
              430.110(A)   pg. 315
              Table 430.250   pg. 322
              Table 240.6(A)   pg. 95

FLC of motor = 27 amperes x 115% = 31.05 amperes
Note – The next standard size circuit breaker is rated 35 amperes.

14. C   392.10(B)(1)(a)   pg. 228

15. B   424.3(A)   pg. 280

16. D   210.64   pg. 66

17. B   220.103   pg. 78
              Table 220.103   pg. 78
              Current formula

18,000 VA x 100% = 18,000 VA
16,000 VA x 75% = 12,000 VA
10,000 VA x 65% = 6,500 VA
        Demand   = 36,500 VA ÷ 240 volts = 152 amperes

18. B   Table 314.16(B)   pg. 176

Size 12 AWG = 2.25 cu. in. x 6 (existing wire in box) = 13.5 cu. in.

   27.0 cu. in. (box volume)
 -13.5 cu. in. (existing wire in box)
   13.5 cu. in. (remaining space)

13.5 cu. in. (remaining space) ÷ 2.5 cu. in. (#10) = 5.4 = 5 wires

19. C   450.13(B)   pg. 335

20. D   430.7(A)(2),(5)&(6)   pg. 298

21. A   500.5(B)   pg. 350

22. D	390.8	pg. 228
23. D	324.41	pg. 185
24. D	690.45	pg. 566
25. C	Chapter 9, Table 5	pg. 685
	Chapter 9, Table 4	pg. 681

Size 1 AWG THW = .1901 sq. in. x 5 = .9505 sq. in.
Size 3 AWG THW = .1134 sq. in. x 5 = .5670 sq. in.
                          Total   1.5175 sq. in.

2½" IMC with an allowable fill of 2.054 sq. in. @ 40% should be selected.

##

TEXAS ELECTRICIANS PRACTICE EXAMS
MASTER ELECTRICIAN
PRACTICE EXAM #13
ANSWER KEY

ANSWER	REFERENCE	NEC PG. #
1. A	3-Phase current formula	

$$I = \frac{kVA \times 1{,}000}{E \times 1.732} \quad I = \frac{150 \times 1{,}000 \text{ VA}}{480 \times 1.732} = \frac{150{,}000}{831.36} = 180.32 \text{ amperes}$$

2. D	Table 310.104(A)	pg. 166
3. B	250.32(B)(1)	pg. 110
	Table 250.122	pg. 125
4. B	Table 310.15(B)(16)	pg. 150
	Table 310.15(B)(2)(a)	pg. 147
	Table 310.15(B)(3)(a)	pg. 148

350 kcmil THW AL ampacity = 250 amperes before derating
250 amps x .82 (temp. correction) x .8 (adj. factor) = 164 amperes

5. C	220.14(I)	pg. 71

120 volts x 20 amperes = 2,400 VA (circuit)
2,400 VA (circuit) ÷ 180 VA (1 receptacle) = 13 receptacles

6. C	411.3	pg. 275
7. D	240.21(B)(1)(1)a.	pg. 96
8. B	Table 310.15(B)(16)	pg. 150
	Table 310.15(B)(2)(a)	pg. 147
	Table 310.15(B)(3)(a)	pg. 148

250 kcmil THWN copper ampacity = 255 amps before derating
255 amps x .82 (temp. correction) x .8 (adj. factor) = 167.28 amperes

9. A	250.24(A)	pg. 107
	250.24(A)(5)	pg. 107
	408.3(C)	pg. 262
10. D	Table 220.55, Column C	pg. 74

35 ranges = 15 kW + 35 kW (1 kW per range) = 50 kW demand

Copyright © 2017

11. B   250.52(A)(4)   pg. 112

12. C   220.82(C)&(C)(4)   pg. 75

   *NOTE - Use the larger of the A/C or heating load.
    25 kW (htr.) + 1.2 kW (blower) = 26.2 kW x 65% = 17.03 kW demand

13. A   220.53   pg. 73

   microwave oven   - 1,250 VA
   trash compactor   -   960 VA
   dish washer   - 1,400 VA
   garage door opener -   960 VA
                         4,570 VA x 75% (demand) = 3,428 VA

14. D   310.15(B)(3), Exception   pg. 148

15. C   Table 344.30(B)(2)   pg. 199

16. D   210.62   pg. 66

17. A   470.3   pg. 340

18. B   700.21   pg. 586

19. D   Chapter 9, Table 8   pg. 689

   $VD = \dfrac{2KID}{CM}$ $VD = \dfrac{2 \times 12.9 \times 90 \text{ amps} \times 225 \text{ ft.}}{52{,}620 \text{ CM}}$ = 9.92 volts dropped

20. D   700.8   pg. 583

21. C   314.28(A)(1)   pg. 180

   2 in. (raceway) x 8 = 16 inches

22. B   250.66(A)   pg. 115

23. A   240.21(B)(3)(1)   pg. 96

24. A   300.20(A)   pg. 141

25. B   680.74(B)   pg. 555

##

Copyright © 2017

TEXAS ELECTRICIANS PRACTICE EXAMS
MASTER ELECTRICIAN
PRACTICE EXAM #14
ANSWER KEY

ANSWER	REFERENCE	NEC PG. #
1. A	250.64(D)(1)(3)	pg. 114
2. A	513.3(C)(1)	pg. 396
3. B Table 310.15(B)(16)	Single-phase current formula pg. 150	

      I = P ÷ E   I = 35,000 watts ÷ 240 = 145.8 amperes
      *NOTE – Size 1/0 AWG THW conductors with an allowable ampacity of 150
   amperes should be selected from Table 310.15(B)(16).

4. A	514.8, Exception 2	pg. 403
5. C	300.4(E)	pg. 135
6. C	230.42(A)(1)	pg. 87
7. A	626.11(A)	pg. 516
8. C	645.5(G)	pg. 527
9. D	Table 220.55 & Notes 1 & 4 Single-phase current formula	pg. 74

   *NOTE - Treat as one range (note 4)
   6 kW + 4 kW + 4 kW = 14 kW total connected load
   14 kW - 12 kW = 2 kW x 5% = 10% increase in Column C (note 1)
   8 kW x 110% (1.1) = 8.8 kW (demand load) = 8,800 watts
   I = P ÷ E   I = 8,800 watts ÷ 240 volts = 36.7 amperes

10. B	511.7(B)(1)(b)	pg. 395
11. D	Table 430.250 430.22 Table 310.15(B)(2)(a) Table 310.15(B)(16)	pg. 322 pg. 302 pg. 147 pg. 150

   25 hp motor FLC = 74.8 amps x 125% = 93.5 amperes
   93.5 amps ÷ .75 (temperature correction) = 124.6 amperes
   *Note - The wire size needs to be increased because of the elevated ambient
       temperature. Size 1 AWG THWN conductors with an ampacity of
       130 amperes should be selected.

Copyright © 2017

12. B	680.62(E)	pg. 555
13. A	511.4(B)(2)	pg. 393
14. D	514.11(A)	pg. 403
15. B	518.4(A)	pg. 435
16. C	450.42	pg. 337
17. B	551.71(B)	pg. 470
18. C	Chapter 9, Table 2	pg. 679
19. A	110.4	pg. 44
20. A	300.7(A)	pg. 138
21. D	Table 310.15(B)(16)	pg. 150
22. C	Table 430.250	pg. 322
	430.24(1)&(2)	pg. 303
	Table 310.15(B)(16)	pg. 150

```
40 hp FLC = 52 amps x 100% = 52 amperes
50 hp FLC = 65 amps x 100% = 65 amperes
60 hp FLC = 77 amps x 125% = 96 amperes
              Total =  213 amperes
```

Size 4/0 AWG THWN copper conductors with an ampacity of 230 amperes should be selected from Table 310.15(B)(16).

23. D	430.53(A)(1)	pg. 309
24. C	680.42(A)(2)	pg. 551
25. C	Chapter 9, Table 8	pg. 689

*Note 3% of 480 volts = .03 x 480 volts = 14.4 (voltage drop permitted)

$$CM = \frac{1.732 \times K \times I \times D}{VD\ permitted}$$

$$CM = \frac{1.732 \times 21.2 \times 100\ amps \times 390\ ft.}{14.4\ volts} = 99,446\ CM$$

*Note - Size 1/0 AWG conductors with a circular mil area of 105,600 CM should be selected.

##

Copyright © 2017

TEXAS ELECTRICIANS PRACTICE EXAMS
MASTER ELECTRICIAN
PRACTICE EXAM #15
ANSWER KEY

ANSWER	REFERENCE	NEC PG. #
1. D	220.14(H)(2)	pg. 71

    100 ft. x 180 VA = 18,000 VA (load)

    120 volts x 20 amperes – 2,400 VA (one circuit)

    $\dfrac{18{,}000 \text{ VA (load)}}{2{,}400 \text{ VA (1ckt.)}}$ = 7.5 = 8 circuits required

2. B	551.73(A)	pg. 471
3. D	240.21(B)&(B)(2)(1)	pg. 96

    100 amperes ÷ 3 = 33.3 amperes

4. D	626.26	pg. 518
5. D	Table 220.12	pg. 71
	220.14(I)	pg. 71
	220.44	pg. 72
	Table 220.44	pg. 72
	Article 100 - Definitions	pg. 35
	230.42(A)(1)	pg. 87

    25,000 sq. ft. x 3.5 VA x 125% (lighting) =   109,375 VA
    150 receptacles x 180 VA each = 27,000 VA
    1st. 10,000 VA @ 100% =   10,000 VA
    27,000 VA - 10,000 VA = 17,000 VA @ 50% =   8,500 VA
                                                 TOTAL = 127,875 VA

6. B	250.24(C)(1)	pg. 107
	Table 250.102(C)(1)	pg. 119
7. C	210.19(A)(1)(a)	pg. 62
	210.11(B)	pg. 60

    400 kVA = 400,000 VA x 125% (continuous load) = 500,000 VA (bldg.)

    277 volts x 20 amperes = 5540 VA (one circuit)

    $\dfrac{500{,}000 \text{ VA. (bldg. lighting)}}{5540 \text{ VA (one circuit)}}$ = 90.2 = 91 circuits

    *NOTE - Circuits need only to be installed to serve the connected load.

Copyright © 2017

8. D	404.8(B)	pg. 256
9. B	501.30(A)	pg. 360
10. C	555.19(A)(4)	pg. 484
11. C	680.23(B)(2)(b)	pg. 547
12. B	450.21(B)	pg. 335
13. B	500.8(E)(1)	pg. 355
14. B	Article 100 - Definitions	pg. 42
15. A	230.44, Exception	pg. 88
16. C	Table 310.15(B)(16) Table 310.15(B(2)(a) Table 310.15(B)(3)(a)	pg. 150 pg. 147 pg. 148

Size 750 kcmil AL ampacity (before derating) = 435 amperes
435 amps x 1.04 (temp. correction) x .8 (adj. factor) = 361.92 amperes

17. D	Table 430.251(A)	pg. 322
18. C	250.30(A)(6)(a)(1)	pg. 109
19. B	250.66 Table 250.66	pg. 115 pg. 116

350 kcmil x 2 conductors = 750 kcmil

*NOTE - A size 4/0 AWG aluminum grounding electrode conductor should be selected from Table 250.66.

20. B	348.20(A)(2)c.	pg. 199
21. B	342.30(A)(2)	pg. 197
22. D	517.19(C)(1)	pg. 422
23. D	388.70	pg. 227

Copyright © 2017

24. D   440.22(A)   pg. 327
25. A   500.7(A)   pg. 352

##

TEXAS ELECTICIANS PRACTICE EXAMS
MASTER ELECTRICIAN
PRACTICE EXAM #16
ANSWER KEY

ANSWER	REFERENCE	NEC PG. #
1. C	700.10(A)(2)	pg. 583
2. C	800.179	pg. 648
3. A	700.12	pg. 584
4. C	517.71(A), Exception	pg. 432
5. B	340.40	pg. 143
6. C	314.28(A)(1)	pg. 180

3 in. (largest conduit) x 8 = 24 in.

7. C	514.8	pg. 403
8. D	Table 430.72(B)	pg. 311
9. C	422.11(E)(3)	pg. 277
	Single-phase current formula	
	Table 240.6(A)	pg. 95

$I = \dfrac{Power}{Volts}$ $I = \dfrac{5{,}000 \text{ VA}}{240 \text{ volts}}$ = 20.8 amperes x 150% = 31.2 amperes

*NOTE - The next standard size circuit breaker with a rating of 35 amperes should be selected.

10. D	300.5(B)	pg. 136
	Table 310.104(A)	pg. 167
	Table 310.15(B)(16)	pg. 150
11. A	110.16(A)	pg. 45
12. B	360.12(6)	pg. 211
13. A	700.12(F)(2)(2)	pg. 585

Copyright © 2017

14. C	430.6(A)(1)	pg. 297
	Table 430.250	pg. 322
	430.52(C)(1)	pg. 307
	Table 430.52	pg. 308

FLC of motor - 46.2 amperes x 250% = 115.5 amperes

15. D	240.83(C)	pg. 100
16. C	388.12(3)	pg. 277
17. A	430.6(A)(2)	pg. 298
	430.32(A)(1)	pg. 304

FLA = 18 amperes x 115% = 20.7 amperes

18. D	450.47	pg. 337
19. B	450.3(B)	pg. 332
	Table 450.3(B)	pg. 333
	Table 240.6(A)	pg. 95
	3-phase current formula	

$$I = \frac{kVA \times 1000}{E \times 1.732} \quad I = \frac{50 \times 1000}{480 \text{ volts} \times 1.732} = \frac{50{,}000}{831.36} = 60.2 \text{ amperes}$$

60.2 amperes x 250% = 150.5 amperes
*NOTE - A 150 ampere OCP device is required.

20. A	502.130(A)(3)	pg. 367
21. D	360.24(A)	pg. 211
	Table 360.24(A)	pg. 211
22. A	502.15(2)	pg. 365
23. D	408.5	pg. 263
24. A	314.71(A)	pg. 182
25. B	Table 300.50, Column 1	pg. 144

##

Copyright © 2017

TEXAS ELECTICIANS PRACTICE EXAMS
SIGN ELECTRICIAN
PRACTICE EXAM #17
ANSWER KEY

ANSWER	REFERENCE	NEC PG. #
1. B	310.10(B)&(C)(2) 300.5(B)	pg. 145 pg. 136
2. A	600.41(B)	pg. 493
3. D	600.6(B)	pg. 489

10 amperes x 2 = 20 amperes

4. B	210.19(A)(1), IN#4	pg. 61

120 volts x 3% = 3.6 volts

5. B	680.57(C)(1)	pg. 554
6. C	600.3 600.10(C)(2)	pg. 488 pg. 490
7. D	Table 300.5, Column 2	pg. 137
8. A	200.6(B) 250.119	pg. 57 pg. 123
9. D	600.4(A)	pg. 488
10. D	600.31(B)	pg. 492
11. B	ANNEX C, Table C.11	pg. 773
12. A	680.57(D) 680.13	pg. 554 pg. 545
13. A	680.57(C)(2)	pg. 554
14. C	600.9(A)	pg. 490
15. B	600.5(B)(2)	pg. 488
16. A	250.148(E)	pg. 127
17. C	230.79(D)	pg. 90

Copyright © 2017

18. B	410.68	pg. 271
19. A	680.57(A)&(B)	pg. 554
20. C	600.5(C)(3)	pg. 489
	410.30(B)(1)	pg. 269
21. D	600.5(B)	pg. 488
22. A	225.7(C)	pg. 79
23. B	Table 310.15(B)(16)	pg. 150
24. B	600.5(A)	pg. 488
25. A	600.6(A)(1)	pg. 489

##

TEXAS ELECTRICIANS PRACTICE EXAMS
SIGN ELECTRICIAN
PRACTICE EXAM #18
ANSWER KEY

ANSWER	REFERENCE	NEC PG. #
1. B	600.21(E)	pg. 491
2. B	600.32(K)	pg. 492
3. A	Trade Knowledge	
4. C	340.10(1)	pg. 195
5. A	600.41(C)	pg. 493
6. D	600.9(C) 410.11	pg. 490 pg. 268
7. B	300.5(D)(1)	pg. 136
8. C	600.10(D)(2)	pg. 490
9. B	600.5(B)(2)	pg. 488
10. A	600.7(B)(7)(1)	pg. 490
11. D	600.21(F)	pg. 491
12. A	314.23(F), Exception 2(2)-(5)	pg. 178
13. D	Article 100 – Definitions	pg. 37
14. C	352.26	pg. 202
15. C	600.5(B)(1)	pg. 488
16. B	225.25(2)	pg. 80
17. A	600.5(C)(3) 410.30(B)(1)	pg. 489 pg. 269
18. D	600.7(B)(4)	pg. 490
19. B	Table 352.44	pg. 203

3.65 in. x 2 = 7.3 inches

| 20. D | 430.33 | pg. 306 |

Copyright © 2017

21. B	Annex C, Table C.4	pg. 731
22. B	600.32(J)(1)(1)	pg. 492
23. C	General Knowledge	
24. B	225.6(A)(1)	pg. 78
25. A	Figure 514.3	pg. 398

##

TEXAS ELECTRICIANS PRACTICE EXAMS
RESIDENTIAL WIREMAN FINAL EXAM
ANSWER KEY

ANSWER	REFERENCE	NEC PG. #
1. B	210.19(A)(3), Exception #1	pg. 62
2. C	210.8(D)	pg. 59
	210.12(A)	pg. 60
3. C	422.13	pg. 277
	422.10(A)	pg. 276
4. B	Table 220.55 & Notes 1 & 4	pg. 74
	334.80	pg. 192
	Table 310.15(B)(16)	pg. 150

17 kW - 12 kW = 5 kW x 5% = 25% (increase in Column C)
8 kW (one appliance) x 1.25 = 10 kW demand (10,000 watts)
I = P ÷ E   I = 10,000 watts ÷ 240 volts = 41.66 amperes
#6 NM cable ampacity = 55 amperes

ANSWER	REFERENCE	NEC PG. #
5. A	550.32(C)	pg. 461
6. B	334.80	pg. 192
7. D	210.52(C)(1)	pg. 65
8. C	314.16(B)(4)	pg. 176
9. D	Article 100 - Definitions	pg. 39
10. A	334.24	pg. 192
11. B	210.19(A)(3)	pg. 62
12. A	314.20	pg. 177
13. A	680.22(C)	pg. 546
14. C	210.8(A)(1),(2)&(3)	pg. 59
15. B	Table 210.21(B)(3)	pg. 63

Copyright © 2017

16. C	334.80	pg. 192
	Table 310.15(B)(16)	pg. 150
	310.15(B)(3)(a)	pg. 147
	Table 310.15(B)(2)(a)	pg. 147
	Table 310.15(B)(3)(a)	pg. 148

30 amps x .91 (temp. correction) x .7 (adj. factor) = 19.11 ampacity

*NOTE - For derating purposes of NM cable the 90 deg. C column of Tbl. 310.15(B)(16) should be used. All conductors are considered current-carrying under this condition.

17. B	300.5(D)(3)	pg. 136
18. C	200.7(C)(1)	pg. 56
19. B	550.32(F)	pg. 462
20. A	250.24(A)(5)	pg. 107
21. D	210.12(A)	pg. 60
22. A	90.5(A)	pg. 31
23. C	230.71(A)	pg. 89
24. B	314.17(C), Exception	pg. 177
25. B	680.22(A)(1)	pg. 546
26. C	334.112	pg. 193
27. A	Table 300.5, Column 5	pg. 137
28. A	210.52(A)(2)(1)	pg. 64
29. B	240.51(B)	pg. 99
30. A	440.62(B)	pg. 329
31. D	410.10(D)	pg. 268
32. D	210.52(C)(1)	pg. 65
33. A	680.21(A)(3)	pg. 545
34. A	Article 100 – Definitions	pg. 35
35. C	210.52(D)	pg. 65
36. B	340.10(3),(4)&(5)	pg. 195
	340.12(1)	pg. 196

Copyright © 2017

37. A	680.42 680.22(A)(1)	pg. 551 pg. 546
38. B	250.102(E)(2)	pg. 119
39. A	410.16(C)(1)	pg. 268
40. D	240.4(D)(7)	pg. 94
41. A	220.53	pg. 73

4,800 VA + 1,200 VA + 1,150 VA + 800 VA + 1,200 VA = 9,150 VA TOTAL
9,150 VA x 75% (demand) = 6,862.5 VA (demand load)

42. C	310.15(B)(7)(1) Table 310.15(B)(16)	pg. 149 pg. 150

175 amperes x 83% = 145.25 amperes
Size 3/0 THWN AL conductors with an ampacity of 155 amperes should be selected from Table 310.15(B)(16).

43. A	424.3(B) 210.19(A)(1)(a)	pg. 280 pg. 62

20 amps / 125% = 16 amps OR 20 amps x 80% = 16 amperes

44. D	210.63, Exception	pg. 66
45. D	310.15(B)(3)(a)	pg. 147
46. C	210.52(C)(5)	pg. 65
47. C	250.66 Table 250.66	pg. 115 pg. 116
48. D	210.11(C)(3)	pg. 60
49. A	210.52(4)	pg. 64
50. C	210.21(B)(1)	pg. 62
51. D	210.52(I)	pg. 66
52. B	210.50(C)	pg. 64

Copyright © 2017

53. B	Trade knowledge

    120 volts x 15 amperes = 1800 VA (one circuit)
    9600 VA (load) ÷ 1800 VA (one circuit) = 5.3 = 6 circuits

54. A	210.52(H)	pg. 66

55. C	220.12	pg. 70

56. D	410.30(A)	pg. 269

57. D	690.7	pg. 560

58. D	314.20	pg. 177

59. B	220.52(A)	pg. 73
    210.11(C)(1)	pg. 60

60. C	550.32(A)	pg. 461

##

Copyright © 2017

TEXAS ELECTRICIANS PRACTICE EXAMS
JOURNEYMAN ELECTRICIANS FINAL EXAM
ANSWER KEY

ANSWER	REFERENCE	NEC PG. #
1. A	230.95	pg. 91
2. B	210.52(C)(2)	pg. 65
3. D	215.3	pg. 68

    240 amps x 125% = 300 amperes

4. B	504.80(C)	pg. 374
5. C	514.9(A)	pg. 403
6. B	225.18(2)	pg. 80
7. A	422.11(E)(3)	pg. 277
8. C	505.7(A)	pg. 377
9. D	Table 314.16(B)	pg. 176
	314.16(B)(1),(2)&(5)	pgs. 175 & 176

```
2 - 6 AWG ungrounded conductors = 2 x 5.00 cu. in. = 10 cu. in.
1 - 6 AWG grounded conductor    = 1 x 5.00 cu. in. =  5 cu. in.
1 - 8 AWG equipt. grounding     = 1 x 3.00 cu. in. =  3 cu. in.
2 - internal clamps             = 1 x 5.00 cu. in. =  5 cu. in.
1 - pigtail                     =     -0-             0 cu. in.
                                        TOTAL    =   23 cu. in.
```

10. C	422.11(C)	pg. 276
11. A	590.6(B)(2)(3)(a)(3)(d)	pg. 487
12. D	300.13(B)	pg. 139
13. C	250.106	pg. 120
14. C	230.26	pg. 86
15. D	300.6(A)	pg. 138

Copyright © 2017

16. D	517.19(A)	pg. 422
17. B	605.9(C)	pg. 496
18. A	230.23(B)	pg. 85
19. B	430.6(A)(2) 430.32(A)(1)	pg. 298 pg. 305

      16 amperes x 125% = 20 amperes

20. C	440.54(B)	pg. 329
21. C	680.43(E)(3)	pg. 552
22. B	250.118(5)b.	pg. 122
23. A	680.26(B)(2)	pg. 549
24. D	220.12	pg. 70
25. B	332.108	pg. 190
26. A	430.14(A)	pg. 301
27. C	300.7(A)	pg. 138
28. B	Table 310.15(B)(16) Table 310.15(B)(3)(a)	pg. 150 pg. 148

      Size 10 AWG THHN ampacity (before derating) = 40 amperes
      40 amperes x 50% (adjustment factor for 20 wires) = 20 amperes

29. B	400.22 & 22(F)	pgs. 250 & 251
30. B	605.9(B)	pg. 496
31. C	Table 210.21(B)(3)	pg. 63
32. D	Table 430.248 Table 430.250	pg. 321 pg. 322
33. B	110.14(C)(1)(b)(1)	pg. 45
34. C	Table 430.250 430.24(1)&(2)	pg. 322 pg. 303

      10 hp - FLC = 30.8 amperes x 125% = 38.5 amperes
      7½ hp - FLC = 24.2 amperes x 100% = <u>24.2 amperes</u>
                        TOTAL   = 62.7 amperes

Copyright © 2017

35. A	210.8(A)(7)	pg. 59
36. A	410.68 Table 310.104(A)	pg. 271 pg. 167
37. A	210.8(B)(2)	pg. 59
38. C	240.24(F)	pg. 99
39. C	250.64(E)(1) 250.106	pg. 115 pg. 120
40. A	Table 300.5, Note 2	pg. 137
41. D	800.53	pg. 640
42. D	220.14(H)(2)	pg. 71
43. D	240.4(B)(1)(2)&(3)	pg. 94
44. B	360.12(6)	pg. 211
45. C	300.4(D)	pg. 135
46. D	Table 310.15(B)(16)	pg. 150
47. B	310.15(B)(3)(a)	pg. 147
48. D	230.2(B)(2)	pg. 84
49. A	680.23(A)(5)	pg. 547
50. A	240.21(B)(3)(1)	pg. 96
51. A	422.5(A)(1)	pg. 276
52. D	440.52(A)(3)	pg. 328
53. D	300.22(B)	pg. 142
54. B	700.5(A) 701.5(A)	pg. 582 pg. 587
55. B	400.14	pg. 250
56. A	550.10(A) & (C)	pg. 455
57. A	250.53(H)	pg. 113
58. C	Chapter 9, Table 1	pg. 689
59. D	800.25	pg. 639

Copyright © 2017

60. A   Chapter. 9, Table 8   pg. 689
Single-phase voltage drop formula

$$VD = \frac{2 \times K \times I \times D}{CM} \quad VD = \frac{2 \times 12.9 \times 10 \times 60}{4{,}110} = \frac{15{,}480}{4{,}110} = 3.76 \text{ volts}$$

#	Ans	Reference	Page
61.	D	300.4(G)	pg. 136
62.	C	430.7(A)(1),(2)&(5)	pg. 298
63.	B	680.34	pg. 551
64.	C	410.30(B)(1)	pg. 269
65.	B	225.6(B)	pg. 79
66.	A	Table 310.15(B)(3)(a)	pg. 148
67.	D	Table 200.55, Column C	pg. 74
68.	D	680.23(A)(4)	pg. 547
69.	C	430.6(A)(2)	pg. 298
70.	B	Note 7 to Chapter 9 Tables	pg. 679
71.	C	300.9	pg. 139
		310.10(B) & (C)	pg. 145
72.	D	Table 310.15(B)(16)	pg. 150
		240.4(B)(1),(2)&(3)	pg. 94
		Table 240.6(A)	pg. 95
73.	B	Chapter 9, Table 4	pg. 680
		Chapter 9, Table 5	pg. 685
		Note 7 to Chapter 9 Tables	pg. 679

$$\frac{0.897 \text{ sq. in. (conduit)}}{0.0824 \text{ sq. in. (wire)}} = 10.8 = 11 \text{ wires}$$

#	Ans	Reference	Page
74.	B	250.52(A)(4)	pg. 112
75.	B	210.62	pg. 66

One receptacle is required for each 12 ft. of show window or major fraction thereof therefore, 2 receptacles are required for each 15 ft. of show window.

#	Ans	Reference	Page
76.	D	Table 110.28	pg. 50

77. B	215.4(A)	pg. 68
78. A	300.5(D)(1)	pg. 136
79. D	Table 110.26(A)(1)	pg. 47
80. C	210.52(A)(2)(1)	pg. 64

##

TEXAS ELECTRICIANS PRACTICE EXAMS
MASTER ELECTRICIAN
FINAL EXAM
ANSWER KEY

ANSWER	REFERENCE	NEC PG. #
1. D	Single-phase current Formula Table 310.15(B)(16)	pg. 150

$$I = \frac{Power}{Volts} \quad I = \frac{90,000 \text{ VA}}{240 \text{ volts}} = 375 \text{ amperes}$$

*NOTE - Size 500 kcmil THHW conductors with an allowable ampacity of 380 amperes should be selected.

2. B	3-phase power Formula VA = I x E x 1.732	

VA = 416 amperes x 208 volts x 1.732 = 149.866 VA
149,866 VA ÷ 1,000 = 149.8 kVA

3. A	314.23(F), Exception 2 (2)-(5)	pg. 178
4. D	645.5(A)	pg. 526
5. B	502.10(A)(3)	pg. 365
6. B	430.32(A)(1)	pg. 305
7. C	250.97, Exception 2	pg. 118
8. C	250.118(6)d.	pg. 122
9. A	430.24(1)&(2)	pg. 303
10. A	525.22(A)	pg. 446
11. C	342.28	pg. 197
12. A	430.6(A)(1)	pg. 297

Copyright © 2017

                    Table 430.248   pg. 321
                    Table 240.6(A)   pg. 95

FLC of motor – 24 amperes x 300% = 72 amperes

*NOTE - In this case you must go down to the next standard size nontime-delay fuse with an ampere rating of 70 amperes.

13. C   645.5(G)   pg. 527

14. B   310.15(B)(5)(a)&(c)   pg. 148

15. D   680.43(B)(1)(a)   pg. 552

16. A   Table 314.16(B)   pg. 176
                    314.16(B)(1)(2)&(5)   pgs. 175 & 176

Size 6 AWG ungrounded conductors   - 3 x 5.00 cu. in. = 15.00 cu. in.
Size 6 AWG grounded conductors   - 3 x 5.00 cu. in. = 15.00 cu. in.
Size 8 AWG grounding conductor   - 1 x 3.00 cu. in. = 3.00 cu. in.
Size 12 AWG ungrounded conductors   - 3 x 2.25 cu. in. = 6.75 cu. in.
Size 12 AWG grounded conductors   - 3 x 2.25 cu. in. = 6.75 cu. in.
Size 12 AWG grounding conductor   -   -0-
internal clamps   - 1 x 5.00 cu. in. = 5.00 cu. in.
                                              TOTAL   = 51.50 cu. in.

17. B   314.28(A)(1)   pg. 180

18. D   530.14   pg. 448

19. D   551.73(A)   pg. 471

20. A   517.19(C)(1)   pg. 422

21. B   440.12(A)(1)   pg. 325

22. A   110.26(C)(2)   pg. 48

23. D   Table 310.104(A)   pg. 166

24. C   340.12(1)   pg. 196

25. A   517.64(A)(1),(2)&(3)   pg. 432

26. B   250.66(A)   pg. 115

27. A   500.5(B)   pg. 350

28. B   501.100(A)(1)   pg. 360

29. C   511.7(B)(1)(b)   pg. 395

Copyright © 2017

30. B	300.34	pg. 143
31. A	430.6(A)(2)	pg. 298
	430.32(A)(1)	pg. 304

FLA of motor = 26 amperes x 115% = 29.9 amperes

32. A	502.130(B)(4)	pg. 367
33. A	220.56	pg. 73
	Table 220.56	pg. 75

    14.00 kW - range
     5.00 kW - water heater
     0.75 kW - mixer
     2.50 kW - dishwasher
     2.00 kW - booster heater
     2.00 kW – broiler
  26.25 kW - total connected load x 65% (demand factor) = 17.06 kW

*NOTE - However the NEC® states the demand shall not be less than the two largest pieces of equipment. 14.00 kW + 5.00 kW = 19 kW demand

34. D	511.4(B)(2)	pg. 393
35. B	Table 110.28	pg. 50
36. B	Table 300.5	pg. 137
37. B	352.44	pg. 203
38. A	430.52(C)(3), Exception 1	pg. 307
39. B	3-Phase Current Formula	
	450.3(B)	pg. 332
	Table 450.3(B)	pg. 333
	Table 240.6(A)	pg. 95

(Primary)
$I = \dfrac{VA}{E \times 1.732}$ $I = \dfrac{150,000}{480 \times 1.732} = \dfrac{150,000}{831.36} = 180$ amps x 250% = 450 amperes

(Secondary)
$I = \dfrac{VA}{E \times 1.732}$ $I = \dfrac{150,000}{208 \times 1.732} = \dfrac{150,000}{36.25} = 416$ amps x 125% = 520 amperes

*NOTE - The next standard size overcurrent device is rated 600 amperes.

40. D	460.28(A)	pg. 340
41. A	430.6(A)(1)	pg. 297

Copyright © 2017

- 221 -

	Table 430.250	pg. 322
	Table 430.52	pg. 308
	Table 240.6(A)	pg. 95

FLC of motor = 21 amperes x 150% = 31.5 amperes

*NOTE - In this situation you are required to go DOWN to the next standard size fuses with a rating of 30 amperes.

42. A	300.3(C)(1)	pg. 134
43. A	250.64(A)	pg. 114
44. D	513.3(C)(1)	pg. 396
45. C	502.115(B)	pg. 366
46. B	3-Phase Current Formula	
	445.13(A)	pg. 330
	Table 310.15(B)(16)	pg. 150

$$I = \frac{kW \times 1{,}000}{volts \times 1.732} \quad I = \frac{200 \times 1{,}000}{480 \times 1.732} = \frac{200{,}000}{831.36} = 240.56 \text{ amperes (FLC)}$$

241 amperes x 115% = 277 amperes (required ampacity of conductors)

*NOTE - Size 300 kcmil THWN conductors with an allowable ampacity of 285 amperes should be selected.

47. B	210.13	pg. 61
48. B	220.12	pg. 70
	Table 220.12	pg. 71

1,400 sq. ft. + 1,400 sq. ft. = 2,800 sq. ft. x 3 VA = 8,400 VA

120 volts x 15 amperes = 1,800 VA of one circuit

$$\frac{8{,}400 \text{ VA (load)}}{1800 \text{ VA (one circuit)}} = 4.6 = 5 \text{ circuits total}$$

49. D	220.82(A)	pg. 75
50. C	368.17(B), Exception	pg. 216
51. A	410.116(B)	pg. 272
52. B	110.31	pg. 49
53. A	700.8	pg. 583

Copyright © 2017

54. C	700.12(A)	pg. 584
55. D	240.83(B)	pg. 100
56. D	210.19(A), IN #4	pg. 61
57. D	314.28(A)(1)	pg. 180

    3 in. (largest conduit) x 8 = 24 in.

58. B	408.5	pg. 263
59. B	800.100(D)	pg. 643
60. A	430.22	pg. 302
	Table 430.250	pg. 322
	Table 310.15(B)(2)(a)	pg. 147
	Table 310.15(B)(16)	pg. 150

    25 hp motor FLC = 74.8 amperes x 125% = 93.5 amperes
    93.5 amperes ÷ .75 (temperature correction) = 124.6 amperes

    *NOTE – The wire size needs to be increased because of the elevated ambient temperature. Size 1 AWG THWN conductors with an allowable ampacity of 130 amperes should be selected.

61. C	690.31(C)(1)	pg. 564
62. A	645.15	pg. 528
63. C	515.7(A)	pg. 406
64. D	310.10(H)(1)	pg. 146
65. B	390.4(A)	pg. 227
66. A	352.30(B)	pg. 203
	Table 352.30	pg. 203
67. B	280.3	pg. 131
68. C	Table 326.80	pg. 187
69. C	404.8(A)	pg. 255
70. B	Table 514.3(B)(1)	pg. 400
71. B	360.12(6)	pg. 211
72. C	388.12(3)	pg. 227

Copyright © 2017

73. D	450.43(B)	pg. 337
74. D	250.64(C)(1)	pg. 114
75. A	430.32(A)(1)	pg. 305

Nameplate rating of motor = 15 amperes x 1.15 = 17.25 amperes

76. D	410.136(B)	pg. 274
77. C	Chapter 9, Table 2	pg. 679
78. D	312.6(B)(2) Table 312.6(B)	pg. 172 pg. 174
79. C	332.24(1)	pg. 190
80. D	110.75(D)	pg. 53
81. B	Table 310.15(B)(16) 240.4(B)(3) Table 240.6(A)	pg. 150 pg. 94 pg. 95

Size 4/0 AWG AL conductors rated @ 75ºC ampacity = 180 amperes
Next standard size OCP is rated at 200 amperes.
*NOTE – Sec. 240.4(F) requires secondary OCP on delta-wye transformers.

82. A	Note 9 to Chapter 9 Tables	pg. 679
83. C	250.53(B)	pg. 113
84. C	430.72(B)(2) Table 430.72(B), Column C	pg. 311 pg. 311
85. D	Table 348.22	pg. 200

3 + 1 equipment grounding conductor = 4 conductors total

86. B	215.2(A)(1)(a) Single-phase current formula	pg. 67

Copyright © 2017

Table 310.15(B)(16)   pg. 150

20,000 VA x 100% = 20,000 VA
16,000 VA x 125% = 20,000 VA
          Total = 40,000 VA

$I = \dfrac{power}{volts}$ $I = \dfrac{40,000 \text{ VA}}{240 \text{ volts}}$ = 166.6 amperes

*NOTE – Size 2/0 AWG conductors with an allowable ampacity of 175 amperes should be selected.

87. A	220.84(C)(3)b.	pg. 76
	Table 220.84	pg. 76

8 kW x 12 units = 96 kW (connected load) x 41% (demand) = 39.36 kW

88. D	450.21(A)	pg. 335
89. C	250.68(C)(1)	pg. 116
90. C	110.31	pg. 49
91. A	Table 312.6(B), Column 1	pg. 174
92. D	314.28(E)	pg. 180
93. B	517.18(A)	pg. 422
	517.19(A)	pg. 422
94. B	Annex C, Table C.3	pg. 726
95. B	225.18(2)	pg. 80
96. D	392.20(B)(1)	pg. 230
97. C	470.3	pg. 340
98. C	250.104(A)(2)	pg. 119
	Table 250.122	pg. 125
99. D	250.30(A)	pg. 108
100. B	210.62	pg. 66

##

Copyright © 2017

www.ingramcontent.com/pod-product-compliance
Lightning Source LLC
Chambersburg PA
CBHW081808300426
44116CB00014B/2279